Listening

to

God

By

Christopher Mace, MD

PublishAmerica
Baltimore

First printing

ISBN: 1-4137-3446-4
PUBLISHED BY PUBLISHAMERICA, LLLP
www.publishamerica.com
Baltimore

Printed in the United States of America

Acknowledgment

I would like to acknowledge Pastor George Henderson, who has been my Pastor and friend for forty-eight years. Although not a collaborator on this book, he undoubtedly will find some of his thoughts in these essays. As a Bible expositor true to the Word of God, his teaching has been an immeasurable blessing to me and my family. I thank God for him.

Dedication

This book is dedicated to my wonderful family that God has given me. I have been abundantly blessed with a beautiful wife and five children whom I love deeply and who have patiently put up with me. It is my prayer they will honestly search daily for God's loving will for their lives.

Chapter 1
Lessons from Jerimiah

Do you have difficulty listening? Not hearing, but listening? How long is your attention span? Despite making a conscious effort, I cannot concentrate long enough to hear all the lyrics of a popular song from beginning to end. My mind wanders much too quickly. Trying to listen to a weather report is just as difficult. By the time the meteorologist finishes the preliminaries, my focus has changed, and I have missed the essentials.

Recently, an elderly gentleman came to my office. Although in his latter eighties, he remains energetic, bright, humorous but given to pessimistic thinking. He appeared tanned, healthy and had just returned from the golf course. My mistake was in asking him how his day had gone. He had a litany of problems. His golf game had been off. There were problems with the mooring for his pleasure boat. He proceeded to list three or four other annoyances that had gone awry in his day. An intense man, he has had the good fortune of health, had an excellent executive position in a large company, and had a comfortable amount of wealth.

He had apparently complained about his problems to his wife over lunch. Her response was disturbing to him. After his list of grievances, she simply said, "Wipe your mouth. You're drooling!"

My response to this story was laughter. He joined in. Do you really think she was listening? I suspect she had had many similar conversations over the years and had simply "tuned out" to what this man recognized as self indulgent pity.

A better illustration of listening was demonstrated by my mother's mother. She was a wonderful, exciting, and at times, excitable lady. She loved drama. She also could be a highly emotional drama queen. As a child, I remember walking to her little apartment for a visit and discovering her sitting in front of one of those large, old table-model radios of 1940 vintage. She not only sat in front of it, she sat directly in front of it with a towel, blanket, or some fabric draped over her head and the radio. She had intimate contact with the radio and her program. All extraneous light, noise, and activity was excluded. Her focus was exclusively on the drama at hand, which most likely was a program such as *The Shadow*. (Remember—"Who knows what evil lurks in the hearts of men? The Shadow knows.") It was always great fun to creep up on her, touch her, and hear her scream! Her involvement in the show transported her into the land of radio. She was "tuned in!"

Jeremiah, who was a prophet to the land of Judah, had an intimate relationship with God . He was so "tuned in" that God talked with him and revealed to Jeremiah the terrible future that Judah was going to suffer at the hands of foreigners. The significant problem was that the Israelites had "tuned" God out. In fact, He was so far out of their focus, they were worshiping idols. God had reached the end of His loving patience. Their sin would be judged.

Known as the weeping prophet, Jeremiah underwent persecution, threats, and imprisonment because he delivered God's desires and admonishments to Judah. His prophesies of impending judgment continued for twenty-three years. Although God withdrew His blessings and severely judged Judah, He confessed His everlasting love, gave them promises for the future, and did not desert them.

There were many reasons why they should have listened to God. These remain current, critical reasons why we also need to pay attention to Him. First of all, we need to turn toward Him and listen

because of Who God is.

God patiently revealed Himself to these people. Hear the words of the Lord in Jeremiah 31:35, "He who appoints the sun to shine by day, who decrees the moon and stars to shine by night, who stirs up the sea so that its waves roar—The Lord Almighty is His name. Only if these decrees vanish from my sight," declares the Lord, "will the descendants of Israel ever cease to be a nation before me."

He continues in verse 37, "Only if the heavens can be measured and the foundations of the earth below be searched out will I reject all the descendants of Israel because of all they have done."

He declared Himself the Sovereign One, the Creator, and the Almighty omnipotent, omnipresent One . He expressed all these concepts through His prophet Jeremiah, whom they ignored. (10:12-16) (23:24) (32:17-25,27) (48:15) (51:15-19,51)

Secondly, We must listen

because God loves us and wants to bless us.

God invested His awesome being, His great optimistic love in this sinful people and promised that the day would come when there would be a new covenant with them.

Consider Jeremiah 32:26. God declared His personal relationship to humanity. His words are either reassuring or frightening depending on one's relationship to God.

"I am the Lord.. the God of ALL mankind…
is anything too hard for me?"

The fact that He is God of "all mankind" is sobering. We are reminded that someday *all* will bow before Him. That nothing is "too hard" for Him reminds us that in His strength all things are possible! However, without belief and faith His hand is still. His strong, generous hand of blessing is not raised. Judah missed the blessing and assistance of the only One who could have saved them.

This revelation of His strength and control over all, even the enemy, was made as the Babylonians were literally seizing their Holy City. The enemy, at that very moment, was building ramps up Jerusalem's wall. God did not prevent the Holy City's takeover because of the persistent disobedience and lack of repentance in His people. He knew that the time of realization of sin and of sorrowful repentance would come. He promised to bring them back home from their captivity. They would be His people, and He would have a new covenant with them. History confirms that this happened as God promised and as Jeremiah predicted.

This fact brings us to a third reason to listen to God. He is not only the Lord God Almighty, Creator of the Universe, controller of its natural laws, and the Wondrous One who loves mankind and wishes to bless them, but, as someone has said,

"History is His Story."

He is the God of all mankind. At our point of consideration, He is specifically the God of Israel. We hold His record in our hands today, this record of His dealings in History. God's

Scriptures are His message of love and justice to Israel and to all peoples. He reveals His call and plan for all generations of mankind. His story is not just about man but involves the larger view of good verses evil, right verses wrong, and God verses Satan. It is the history of a raging Spiritual Battle. If we look beneath the surface of recorded facts, we sense the intensity of this battle. *See it in the life of Job! Hear it in the history of Israel! Feel it in the human journey of the Lord Jesus! Be aware of it in your own life! The real story lies behind our story. It is His Story.*

Fourthly, we should listen to God because

God is a personal God.

Jeremiah is a great example of this fact. He was known by God as a special and unique individual. Jeremiah 1:5 tells us:

1.   that God formed him in the womb,
2.   that He knew him before he was born,
3.   that He had set Jeremiah apart and had appointed him as a prophet to the nations.

Obviously, that passage could generate many questions and much serious thought and discussion. However, it is sufficiently evident that God knew Jeremiah as a specific individual and was involved in his life. Furthermore, this truth is obvious in Jeremiah 1:9, which states that God reached out His hand and touched his mouth, giving him words to say. God used Jeremiah as His voice to plead, reason, and prophesy. That God spoke to him personally is notable throughout Jeremiah's prophetic Book. God gave him promises. He told Jeremiah, "Look, my friend, this is not going to be easy."(my paraphrase) They are going to "fight" against you, but "here is the great part, you won't be alone. I am with you, and I will rescue you." (Jeremiah 1:19) Yes, God is the personal God of that individual who will trust Him.

A fifth reason we need to listen to God is

because of Who we are.

Read Jeremiah 10:23. Jeremiah is talking in prayer to the Lord and says, "A man's life is not his own." Consider chapter 17:5. The Lord speaks, "Cursed is the one who trusts in man, who depends upon flesh for his strength, and whose heart turns away from the Lord." Verse 17: 9 tells us, "The heart is deceitful above all things and beyond cure. Who can understand it?" Then He says that, "I, the Lord, search the heart and examine the mind to reward a man according to his conduct."

There are many verses in the Old and New Testaments that point out the pathetic condition of man's soul. These few verses in Jeremiah adequately clue us into the facts that:

1.   Ultimately, we are not in control of our lives. Our life is not our own. We have no power to give life, no power to control life, no power to stop death.
2.   We are weak and untrustworthy.
3.   In our natural state we rebel against God. We are born the rebellious children of Adam. There is no human cure for our spiritual genes.
4.   We stand incomplete, unqualified and inadequate before the examining eyes of God.

However, God always makes loving provision for our natural, sinful state. We are not left in limbo in this desperate, powerless state of condemnation. In this same scripture, God

makes it clear that in a complete and trusting relationship with Him we are
1. blessed (verse 8),
2. will be nourished and will grow like a tree beside the water,
3. need not fear and worry and be fruitless,
4. that we have a place of Sanctuary (verse 12), and
5. and the source of our life is the Lord, the spring of living water (verse 13).

Listening to God is imperative because our very nature needs the Salvation and Life found in Him alone.

We must listen to God!

—not only because of who He is and because He desires a relationship with us and wants to bless us. We need to hear what God has to say not only because He is the God of History, because He is a personal God, because of who we are, and our deep need for His salvation, but—

because He listens to us.

How does he listen? Attentively! In Jeremiah 8:6, God tells us, "I have listened attentively." We know from previous Scripture that God examines the heart and mind. Now understand what He hears, or what He does not hear, when He listens to the hearts and minds of Humanity.

They do not say what is right!
No one repents!
Each pursues his own course!
My people do not know the requirements of the Lord!
They have rejected His Word!

They have no shame, and even the priests and prophets have practiced deceit!

He heard no acknowledgment of His life or saw no evidence of His Work among them. Unfortunately, these statements are as culturally contemporary today as they were for Jeremiah's land of Judah.

We need to listen to Him!

He knows our deepest, essential needs and is the source of rest and comfort and healing. He is the Balm of Gilead and the healing salve for the wounded spirit. However, He will not perform His work in ungrateful, unbelieving hearts.

A difficult lesson to learn is that the Pursuit of Happiness is really the Pursuit of God. God has our best interests at heart. Hear His anguish and seeming disappointment shown in Jeremiah chapter 3:19, "How gladly would I treat you like sons and give you a desirable land, the most beautiful inheritance of any nation. I thought you would call me Father and not turn away from me..."

God wanted an intimate relationship with Israel. He had abundant blessings and love to lavish on His family. The stubborn, unenlightened, rebellious heart challenges God's right to acknowledgment, to worship, and to obedience. We miss **God's blessing of His best for us** when we do not submit to what is right for us. He is the authority on morality and civility. Equality, justice, love, and happiness for all are His domain.

Seventh, we need to listen to Him because

what He says is true. He does not lie.

Absolute Truth is found in the Word of God. We are grateful for those who teach us. But even in Jeremiah's day, the priests were prophesying lies and were ruling by their own authority, not God's! The religious teachers were said to be godless and to have taken evil courses! Chapter 23:26 sadly reveals that some of the nonreligious officials knew more about God than the priests and prophets. This problem has persisted through the ages to the present day when religious proponents of vain philosophies lead people astray by tickling the intellect. They appeal to faulty logic, secular reasoning, or even just to our emotions. Ignorance and unfamiliarity with God's doctrines will lead to deluded thinking. We have the Scriptures. We need to explore them.

John tells us in his second epistle "anyone who runs ahead and does not continue in the teaching of Christ does not have God."

Our faith must be based on the revealed Word of God. Heb 1:1-3 reveals, "He has spoken to our forefathers through the prophets at many times and in various ways, but in these last days He has spoken to us through His Son, through whom He made the Universe, who is the radiance of God's glory and the exact representation of His being, sustaining all things by His powerful Word." Can one doubt the importance of Christ and His words?

Judah chose to follow faulty wisdom and humanistic thinking. God asked for obedience to His powerful, infallible Word. He had delivered His Word to Israel, the nation whom He had chosen to convey His Truths to other peoples. He had ordained them as His special people through whom He would speak and reveal Himself to others. He had trusted this nation with His presence, His Word, His blessings, His leaders, the Patriarchs, and the Covenants. How could He speak through them unless they listened and were attentive to His voice and activity?

Today the Church is the vehicle for God's voice to the world. If that is true, it is imperative that The Church listen to and clearly convey His message to this needy place. Jesus Himself was called the Word. (John 1, Rev. 1) Christ is the full expression of the Father. He is the expression of God's love. His words were from God. That we are acquainted with this One called the Word is more than important. It is vital.

Wisdom comes from the Word. In the parable of the wise and foolish man, Christ taught that those who heard and practiced His teachings were like the wise man, safe on the Rock in the times of storm.

Salvation is found in the Word. Literally salvation is found in Christ, the living Word. The Apostle Paul explained that in order to believe, people must hear, and to hear they must have a preacher, and the preacher must be sent. (Rom 10:14) Unequivocally, hearing the written Word is essential for Salvation.

To those who hear and believe, **the Word cleanses**. It is the inculcation of the Word into the fabric and framework of our spiritual beings that leads to repentance and Holy living. We are clean through the Word.

We know that **the Word of God illuminates**. It is a light unto our paths and a lamp unto our feet. (Psalm 119) We need its instruction and guidance.

One of the more interesting and deeply sobering reasons to listen to God is what Jesus taught regarding His Words in John 13:48. He stated that He had not come to judge (He came to "seek and to save" that which is lost) but that **those who reject Him and His Words will be condemned by His very Words**. Jesus further states (verse49), "For I did not speak of my own accord, but the Father who sent me commanded me what to say and how to say it. I know that His command leads to eternal life."

If we believe in Jesus Christ and hear those words, we are obligated to listen and learn what He said. Heb 4:12 tells us that **His words are "living" and "powerful" and "sharp" and "penetrating" and " judge" the thoughts and attitudes of the heart.**

Many interferences obstruct attempts to keep "tuned in" to God and the Scriptures. By nature we lack focus and interest. This fact explains the trouble we have heeding God. We may miss a blessing or sustain more dire consequences because of distractions. We all can remember personal instances of disobedience or unfaithfulness and the consequences of missed blessings or of God's chiding.

Consider some of the consequences and lessons learned from Biblical persons. Some suffered the outcomes of not listening, others reaped the benefits of being "tuned in."

For instance, Eve switched the channel to the "other station" and preferred listening to the channel of "other voices" which appealed to her emotion. She valued these voices above the Word of God and made a disastrous, faulty decision based on Satan's deceitfulness. Adam's and Eve's decisions corrupted all future human generations, which have been born with a naturally rebellious nature that does not listen to God easily.

Saul, the King of Israel, decided not to adhere to God's instructions. He disobediently kept the spoils of war and did not completely annihilate the Amalekite nation as God had ordered. He thought his plan better than God's. His favorite channel was the channel of "Humanistic Thinking." Saul went his arrogant way and ended up far from God.

Ananias and Sapphira tuned to the channel of "delusion and

deceit." Deception conveniently went along with what they had chosen to do. Although they easily deceived others, God knew. Lying brought them sudden, premature deaths. (Acts 5)

Judas literally sat at the feet of Jesus for three years. His attention span must have been very short. He saw the miracles. He listened to the teachings. At one point, he had the power to perform miracles. He knew the Lord Jesus Christ in person but never allowed Christ's voice to penetrate his greedy heart that was left open to promptings from Satan and eventually inhabitation by Satan. He failed to dial to the channel of "Truth" but flipped to that of "unbelief and greed." Thirty pieces of silver were more valued than friendship with the Holy Master of the Universe and the salvation of his soul. At his end he suffered despair and death at his own hand.

Some Biblical personalities had lapses in their concentration. They flipped to easy listening channels that espoused a different world view from God's, or they just tuned out for a while. But they eventually retuned to the "Fellowship of God" channel.

Another King, David, chose to listen to the tunes of "lust and willful disobedience." His family reaped sad consequences, but David repented and was restored to fellowship with God.

There are many accounts of those who stayed the course. People who listened to the channel of "Faith, Hope and Charity."

Moses, that great leader of the Israelites, led his nation from Egyptian captivity and knew the miracle of salvation at the Red Sea. God had revealed himself to Moses in the burning bush and in special revelations on Mount Sinai. Moses' face had glowed with God's glory after he had been with Him. He was the privileged inscriber of the moral and religious laws. A lapse in attitude had sad consequences and prevented him from experiencing the promised land. But he died in the presence, if not the arms, of God. (Deuteronomy 34)

Think of Gideon who conquered a massive enemy with three-hundred soldiers. He checked "God's Channel" a few times to see if he was getting the right reception by asking specific feats from God. Undoubtedly, he had been tempted to listen to the "logic channel" of battle advisors and their strategies. But he stayed tuned to God, who willingly proved Himself to Gideon. Can you imagine going into battle against an overpowering enemy force with only bugles, torches, and pitchers as weapons!? Gideon focused on the channel of "God's Way" and won the victory.

Think of Thomas. After all night prayer, the Lord picked him as one of his special, chosen disciples to whom he would teach and demonstrate His Godliness. Although Thomas appeared to be a man of reason and logic, he was given to pessimism. Like all of us, he heard Jesus through the filter of his personality and a mind corrupted by humanistic thinking. Not much is said in the Scriptures about Thomas. John tells us the most. Thomas was present when Jesus received the news of Lazarus's illness. He heard Jesus' decision to wait three days before responding to Mary and Martha's sad but confident cry for their Friend to come and heal Lazarus.

Christ knew what an ageless opportunity this occasion presented to honor God and reveal to centuries of believers the fact that He is the Resurrection and the Life. All life exists because of Him and New Life begins in Him. He is the Almighty who has power over death. He would demonstrate that in a profound and vivid manner. But that Truth was not a foremost concern to Thomas who tried to dissuade the Lord from going to what seemed certain death and persecution from the authorities. Thomas grudgingly gave in by saying (my paraphrase), "Oh, ok, boys, let's go and die with Him."

There is a hint of courage in those words but certainly not much evidence of faith in the Master. Thomas not only lived to get to Judea but saw the miracle of Lazarus' resurrection. Christ always shows Himself faithful.

Next, Thomas is discovered in the upper room the night of Christ's betrayal. He was blessed by having his feet washed by the Savior. He listened to the teaching of Christ that night. And yet he did not understand. That last night, Christ told them that He would be leaving them, and they could not come with Him. He then said He was "the Way, the Truth, the Life and that they knew the Way." Thomas had a very logical, but certainly not obviously perceptive, question in the context of recent events and teaching, "How can we know the way? We do not even know where you are going?" (I am not being critical of Thomas as I can imagine myself thinking similarly.)

The next time we search for Thomas, he can't be found. He is missing from Christ's first post resurrection appearance to his disciples. Ironic isn't it that Christ had shown and taught that He was the Resurrection and the Life, and Thomas did not believe? Had he really seen? Had he really listened? He refused to accept this teaching until he saw the Risen Savior. But sight dispelled all doubt. He fell before Christ and confessed Him as Lord and God. All suspicion was gone forever. Events proved that.

The last time we catch sight of Thomas, he is in the same room as the other Disciples after Christ had ascended into the Heavens. Doing what? Praying now to the One he could not see, or touch, or feel. He now trusted and believed and awaited the One that Christ was to send to them as Comforter, Teacher, and Guide. Thomas had moved beyond doubt to belief as an ardent active disciple who later became a Missionary to both the near and Far East. He died in India as a martyr for the cause of the Gospel. His own personality no longer interfered. He heard clearly the clarion voice of the Master as Christ departed this earth, "Go Ye into all the World." He had changed from listening to programs of "doubt and skepticism" to those of "the power of belief in action."

The Faith chapter, Hebrews 11, is filled with names of men and women who tuned into the channel of "God's Faithfulness" and believed. This chapter is not as much about men's faith in God as it is of God's faithfulness to men and women. They were not perfect but were willing to listen to God's voice at crucial times in their lives and to participate in His plan.

There are many reasons for losing focus and not listening attentively. Callousness, hardness of heart, mental fatigue, distractions, or busyness dull our spiritual hearing and blur our vision. We become either spiritually lazy or spiritual tired. The answer to our lassitude lies in the strength of our relationship. Do we abide in the Father? Are we listening to "The Word of Life Channel?" Do we recognize the significance of the God's Word which will judge us?

John 3:16 affirms to us that Christ is the way to everlasting life. Either we are on that way or on some other way that does not lead to everlasting life.

Christ taught that if we are to be His kin (His Mother and His brother) then we must be those who hear and put into practice God's Word. (Luke 8:21) So, either we have a close relationship with Him or we don't. The intimacy of that relationship depends on our hearing God and acting upon His Word. This idea that practicing what God says is what confirms our relationship to Christ is restated slightly differently in Luke 6:27. Christ said, "Hear me," and gave familiar instructions.

Love your enemies.
Do good to those who hate you.
Bless those who curse you.
Pray for them that mistreat you.
Do unto others as you would have them do unto you.

Then He told his disciples their reward would be great if there was obedience. He didn't say that they would feel good and that everyone would like them and think that they were great guys! But He did say they would be "sons" of the Most High God. Their reward was the kinship to the Heavenly Father and the Only Begotten Son.

So, either we are part of His family or we aren't!

ARE WE LISTENING?

Not only is the Word of God important in our Salvation, and in our Relationship to God, **Scripture is our primary defense** against the fiery darts of the devil. The Lord Jesus answered the temptations in the wilderness with the Word of God. Those of you who have read *Pilgrim's Progress* will remember that Christian met the ugly Dragon in the Valley of Humility and answered each onslaught in that satanic battle with the Word of God. The Scripture is our stabilizer in days of depression, in times of temptation, and in our materialistic, humanistic society that denies the need of God, if not God Himself.

Either we will fall defeated or stand victorious depending on how deeply we are embedded in the knowledge of God's Word.

Luke 8:18 exhorts us to consider how we listen. Do we hear? Do we listen with understanding and determination? "Whoever has will be given more. Whoever has not, even what he thinks he has, will be taken away."

If we do not understand and appropriate Truth, it will be lost.

We will either receive or lose the blessings of the promises and instructions of God.

Therefore, important reasons to honor the Holy Bible in our lives include its role in our Salvation, in our relationship to God, in our strength and defense for victorious living, and in the knowledge and blessing it brings to us.

Tune in to this lively drama. There is nothing common about you or me! As spiritual beings we trace our ancestry to that great and glorious moment in time called creation. We have faced the tragedy of a lost estate that has suffered disruption in its communication with God. We are part of a rebellious tribe that for centuries has yearned to repair this relationship but can not find the way back to God. Deaf, blind and naked, we have cloaked ourselves in self-righteousness but know the dirtiness of heart and minds that only God can see. We have failed to control ourselves and our destinies. Ultimately, we know failure and death. We futilely struggle to keep the moral and ethical codes of God (the Law) and society only to be burdened with guilt and knowledge of our inadequacy for good. We recognize that we can not personally bridge the great gulf between us and God. We have witnessed the humble, glorious entrance of the Very Creator of the Universe and the Living Expression of God into the chaos of the human condition. Having followed Him through his earthy trial, we have misunderstood Him, not recognized Him, and disbelieved Him. We have seen Christ on the cross of Calvary. After His innocent, bitter death, we experienced His wondrous victory over death at the empty tomb. Our sad condition pointed out our need for His wonderful Salvation. We have known the whisper of the Spirit of God in our lives. Those who chose to trust Him have received Heavenly blessings of grace, joy, unconditional love and His faithful presence. We have listened to God's love story. But have we really heard how special we are? Is there too much static? Has there been interference in our reception? Have we been tuning the dial to matters that we consider more pressing than God or to distractions that take the focus away from God and allow us to indulge in selfish emotions, thoughts, philosophies and behaviors for a season? Ecclesiastes reminds us that all is vanity, everything is soap bubbles, everything will pass away except the things of God. The remarkable but undeniable conclusion of this ancient Book is, "It is the sole duty of man to seek God and keep His commandments—."

Those thoughts bring us back to Jeremiah. The malady in that day was disobedience. The people were arrogant. They chose to rest in logic and not faith. They had no trust in God or knowledge of His desires for them. They had no teaching. They would not repent or even listen. On one occasion they came to Jeremiah regarding a certain issue and asked him to seek God's face about it. (42:2-3) When Jeremiah reported God's answer, they flatly rejected it and did as they wanted. They actually said, "We will not listen."

On a number of occasion the scriptures report that the people did not listen, or they did not hear. Once God spoke to them, but they did not listen. He called to them, but they did not answer. (Jeremiah 35:17) He turned up the volume! How He amplified His message isn't stated. Whether it was through the speaking, preaching and crying of His prophets or through the especially grim circumstances that affected that country isn't clear, but he tried to get their attention. They would not listen. There was too much static in their busy, selfish, pagan lives and too much interference in their relationship for God to get through.

We cannot obey Him unless we know what He wants in our lives. The simple truth is that in order to hear Him we must sit with Him, mediate on Him, talk with Him, and focus on His revealed truth and its applications to us. Then we will hear with our souls and Trust and Obey. We will be "tuned in," not "out," to the "Voice of Heaven," not the "Voice of Maine." The dials of our hearts and mind must be permanently tuned to worship. God is more than a Heavenly talk show host. He attentively listens and responds generously in His abundant grace and omniscient wisdom accomplishes the best good for us in any and all circumstances. If we recognize and trust Him, we will enlarge our knowledge, increase His presence in our lives, and expand our vision of Him and what He desires of us.

One final reason to listen to this Heavenly Voice is because

someday we will see Him.

Hopefully, we will see Him as our Savior. Without that belief and trust in Him as Savior and God, we would have no right to a relationship with the Father. This God of History is also **the God of Eternity**. Someday it is promised that we will dwell with Him based on our trust in Him.

Paul's prayer of Eph 1:17-18 asks the God of glory to enlighten the Ephesians so they would know what He is calling them to do or be. He is calling each of us into a saving, loving relationship with Him.

Are we looking for the evidence of God's work in our lives? Will we willingly participate in His will? Are we acknowledging God in our lives? Are we too preoccupied with the things of earth? Do we hear God's voice filtered through the earmuffs of our own desires, misunderstandings, slothfulness, circumstances, traditions, and preconceived notions. Jeremiah 42:19 claims that **"the people made a fatal mistake. They had knowledge of the truth and chose to disobey."** Listening is a choice that takes work and concentration! But if we do not hear, we will not believe, and if we do not believe, we will not have a vision. We will live life to its fullest potential only in the plan of God and with the power of God's Spirit. If we have no vision, others will perish. Will we hear the sad cry of Judah? "The summer has ended, and we are not saved." (Jeremiah 8:20) Will that be our personal cry? Or will we weep with those who did not learn of Salvation because we would not hear God's call to personal obedience and Holiness?

Hear God's words of command and comfort:

Believe on the Lord Jesus Christ and you will be saved.

For God so loved the World that He gave His only begotten Son that whosoever believeth in Him shall not perish but have everlasting life.

I am the Way, the Truth, and the Life- no man comes to the Father but by me.

Come unto me all ye that labor and have heavy burdens and I will give you rest.

Take up your cross and follow me.

Seek ye first the Kingdom of God and all these things shall be added unto you.

I am the Good Shepherd and I take care of my sheep.

I am with you always.

Be ye Holy even as I am Holy.

Let your light shine before men that they will see your good works and glorify your Father who is in heaven.

Go ye into all the world and preach the gospel to every creature.

Love your neighbor as yourself.

Love each other for by this will all men know that you are mine. (paraphrase)

I will come again and receive you unto myself that where I am there ye may be also.

These are old and familiar sayings, but have we heard them? Have we heard them? Has their true meaning penetrated our minds and beings so that we are changed forever? The tone of our earthly lives and the tenor of our eternal destiny hinge on Christ's words and our response to them. We will be saved for eternity or sunk forever in hell. We will live robed in Christ's righteousness or die in our own rags of self righteousness. We will have an intimate family relationship as heirs of God and co-heirs with Christ or be self deluded with an illegitimate false family facade. We will be illuminated or we will be ignorant. We will be servants or we will be selfish. We will either stand on the mighty promises or sit in the pathetic prison of anxiety and fear. We will be victorious, or we will be victimized.

So, are we, as Christian did in *Pilgrim's Progress*, keeping focused on the Word, reveling in the Promises, and constantly keeping in mind eternity and its values and searching the way ahead for the distant light of the Celestial City?

Stayed tuned to God because of Who He is:

because He loves us, wants a relationship with us and desires to bless us;
because He is the God of History and gives meaning to time;
because He is a personal God who knows us and our deep need of Him;
because He listens to us;
because what He has to say is eternally important;
because the consequences of not listening will be severe;

because we will be judged by His Word;
because we will see Him someday.

Remember the story of my grandmother and her attempt to be completely focused and be rid of distractions. Stay tuned and, as the old hymn expresses it, "the things of earth will grow strangely dim in the light of His glory and grace." Dwell in the Word in worship and in communion with the Savior. Construct a solid faith. Participate in fellowship with other believers.

After identifying who Christ is, the author of Hebrews tells us, "We must pay more careful attention so we do not drift away." (Heb 2:1) We have been distracted! We are falling asleep at the dial. Let's get a cup of spiritual caffeine and turn up the volume. Don't drift away because the rest of that message is, "How shall we escape if we neglect so great a salvation?"

Fight the fight. Run the race. Glorify God. The reward is ahead. For now we must listen intently and quietly to the One who knows all things. Listen and hear! Look and see! In a word, BELIEVE— deep down in your soul where it will make a difference for you and others.

There has been a Great Sacrifice made for us. God gave His best. Christ gave His all. The price has been paid for everyone. And yet there is great cost if we do not listen. That cost is personal. It is both current as well as future. Our journey in time is short. The Word of God guides us in the everlasting Way. The Expressed Word of God, Jesus Christ, who said, "I am the Door," is the gate into the Heavenly City.

Listen daily to His wise and tender voice. Even when the din of life is almost too much, you will hear Him calling you.

Chapter 2
Listening to the Savior
(Listening With a Needy Heart)

Recently I recommended to a new friend that he should study the Book of John if he wished to know the true Biblical Christ. The hope was that he might gain a different perspective than his own ideas about who Christ was. After that suggestion, reevaluating John's presentation of Christ became a personal goal of mine.

The ease with which Christ engaged himself with others is intriguing. Often times he introduced Himself by asking a question or by making a statement. His ultimate goal seemed to be to stimulate an introspective search that would lead to a deeper knowledge of self and the need for a relationship with Christ and the Father.

Prior to the events of the text at which we will look, Christ had met a number of individuals, had delivered some profound teaching and had demonstrated the nature of His character as well as that of the Father.

He told Nicodemus, a devout Rabbi, that he needed to be "born again" if he wanted to see the Kingdom of God. Such an incredulous statement took Nicodemus off guard. He was surprised into considering a different perception of the profound truths of God's love and dealings with mankind. He was challenged with new thinking and with views he had not previously considered. In that encounter with Christ, this Rabbi learned the basic explanation of the Gospel, the reason for Christ's earthly existence, and the true nature of God's heart. John 3:16 was spoken directly to him. The very Son of God gave him those words to ponder. Generations have joyfully repeated these words for twenty centuries. We memorized them as young people. They are the words of Truth and Hope to which all Christians cling.

Christ had a simple question for the woman at the well, "Will you give me to drink?" This ordinary request had an extraordinary reaction. It exploded into many questions and cascaded from a cultural dilemma over the difficult relationship between the Samarians and the Jews to a religious discussion and eventually into a riveting personal revelation that was pivotal in this woman coming to know Christ. What happened after that may have been the first open air evangelistic campaign. The Sovereign God of the universe was the Teacher. That woman's village came to hear Him and was changed not only because of her testimony but because of individual personal interactions with the Savior.

Christ spoke abruptly and almost accusingly to the father of the sick dying child. The father, a royal official, had begged Christ to come and heal his son. Jesus had said "Unless you people see miraculous signs and wonders, you will never believe." (John 4:48) This declaration seems to fly in the face of the Official who had humbled himself by requesting help from Christ, who was socially inferior to him.

Undoubtedly, Christ's tone was not harsh, but he delivered this consideration in a thought-provoking manner as a gentle request for the father's affirmation of faith. He was asking if this man really believed in Him or did he want to use Christ for his own purposes?

The Official showed faith and persistence in his repeat request "Sir, come down before my child dies..." One can hear the urgency. But one can also hear the certainty of his belief. Christ refused to go with the Official to see his son and forced a further demonstration of the Official's faith in Him. Christ told him to go and that his son would live. Probably anxiously, the Official left the Great Physician but accepted His Word. His faith was great, but it grew more that day as he walked into the unknown, accepting what the Savior had told him. Sometimes Christ's verbal approach to people may have seemed unkind. But if we listen closely, we detect the loving tone of His voice.

John 5:1-14 presents the text of The Healing of the Invalid at the Pool of Bethesda. Christ presented a very intriguing question to this poor, unfortunate man. The astounding question asked by Christ was "Do you want to get well?"

Any health care provider can understand that question. There are many health problems for which patients tend to avoid taking responsibility. We refuse to relinquish unhealthy habits and lifestyles. We want to be well, but we do not eat correctly, exercise, or take our medications properly. We do not want the consequences of our behaviors but are not willing to participate in our own wellness. Such behavior is also typical of us spiritually. We want joy and peace and spiritual wholeness but hold onto our bitterness, our fear, our anger, our pride and our own way. Many times we ignore the long-term effects of our choices.

Christ's conversation with this paralyzed man raises some concerns. How might I have responded to such a question? Would I have been indignant? After all, superficially this seems an insensitive, outlandish question. Imagine it! This man had been paralytic for thirty eight years. He was too immobile to hobble into the water at the time of healing. He had to have felt alone and deserted with no one to assist him. He did not know who Jesus was, let alone understand His ability to cure him. That Christ was a stranger is obvious because when the authorities questioned the man about who had healed him the man could not tell them.

Would I have been indignant and have responded in an ungracious way to Jesus? Would I have impolitely asked Christ if He had trouble with His vision? Couldn't He see? Couldn't He understand? Did He need to mock him? Did He think he was just a lazy beggar? What kind of an idiot would ask that kind of a question? If I had been listening, would my eyebrows have been raised in criticism because of this derogatory, hurtful statement to this unfortunate man?

However, as we consider the scene, the realization comes that this very sick man has the powerful Creator of the Universe focused on him. He is the very One who had told Nicodemus that God loved the world. He was the one chosen to save the world. Can you envision Christ bending over him now, maybe even kneeling and touching him lightly. His soft voice filled with interest and concern asks permission to come into the presence of this societal cast off. Does this remind us of how Christ has come into our lives? There is no forcing, just a request "Do you want to be well? Do want to accept my forgiveness for your crippling sins? Do you want to be cured from your devastating burdens and pains that leave you lonely and empty and without help apart from God?"

Christ approaches His Saints as tenderly as those who do not recognize Him. "Do you want to be whole? You need to hear my Word, be obedient to the principles of new life and let go of your attitudinal and behavioral sins." Doesn't that remind you of the way he deals with us who are the spiritually crippled?

This invalid must have seen compassion in those Godly eyes and heard love and power in the sweet voice that could speak to the raging winds and seas and quiet them and could with just a word give movement to lame and paralyzed limbs and sight to darkened eyes, and life to dead bodies and spirits. He must have recognized in the question of "Do you want to be well?" that there was an implied answer of "I can help you! I am able" because the invalid answered with respect and rationalization. He explained that he could not help himself and he had no one to administer to him. He needed a savior, one who could take him to the place of healing and wholeness. His answer was a hopeless answer. He had been trying. He recognized his helpless state but was alone with his problem, ineffective, unable, inadequate. The spiritual application is obvious. We are lost apart from the Jesus Christ's offer to make us well. This invalid personally experienced the life giving words of Christ. He was to know the power of them. It was not a touch or an act performed by Christ but it was His Word that healed this man. It is the same for those who listen. We are clean through the Word. We are free through the truth. "Ye shall know the truth and the truth will make you free."

"Do you want to get well?" That original question had a deeper meaning for this man. It was not just a request for permission to enter into this man's life. Rather it raised another question of whether he really wanted to be changed? There are consequences to your decision. You will be healed. You will be in a far better condition. Your life will have greater meaning, but it will not be easy.

After the healing, his life would be completely changed. He could have a different life style now. He would need a different job. His income was gone because he was a beggar. The very reason for his existence would be called into question. Imagine how his needs would change. He had access to so much more of life now. How would he adjust and manage to meet those wants and needs? His identity would be different. He had a new physical life but also a new spiritual being was born as well. He had met the God of the universe and did not know it? But time revealed that fact to him in his second encounter with Christ when his spirit was forever changed. (John 5:14)

Do we want spiritual healing? Are we truly prepared to go this path of change? Salvation means that we are new creations. We have new life. We have been changed. The old life is gone. We are regenerated, newly related to the Heavenly Father. That is the teaching of Scripture.

"Choosing to be well" is not always the choice we make. Some of us have heard the words of and about the Savior: "Come unto me." "I am the Way." "Whosoever will may come." "Believe on the Lord Jesus and you shall be saved."

Some hear the Good News and reject it. Consider Judas, who had been personally chosen by the Lord and had spent three years in the Clinic of the Great Physician. He incredibly chose not to be well, not to be a true disciple of Christ, and betrayed the One who, humbly kneeling before him, had washed his feet just hours before that betrayal. Judas suffered a bitter, disillusioned end.

About a year ago a patient who had been living in California and had been diagnosed with cancer returned home to deal with this issue and to ultimately die. We addressed his physical needs, but the attempt was futile. He was a peach of a man, a sensitive, intelligent, kind, interesting man who enjoyed books, gardening, and good food. He had not given God much thought or time. We talked about Faith and Christ and the Gospel. He felt it would be wrong for him in his dying days to seek God's face because he had ignored God during his life. His thinking led us to the parable of the farmer who repeatedly went back to the town square looking for laborers to work in his vineyard. He contracted for certain wages with the hired help who went to work for him early in the morning. However, he returned to the village at different intervals looking for more help. Each time he hired more workers. At the end of the day he paid every one the same wages even though some had worked much shorter times than those hired early in the day.

We explored the fact that God's grace is fully extended and as wonderfully rewarding to those who enter His Kingdom in the latter hours as those who spend their whole lives there. But to my knowledge that man's pride prevented him from being spiritually whole. He never accepted God's offer. He chose not to be well.

Consider also some who have chosen to take the path of healing and the consequences of their decision. What would the world be like if the Disciples had not chosen inward healing? What if they had chosen not to respond to Christ's challenge of, "Follow me"? What would their lives have been like if they had not endured three years trudging around the Holy Land with the itinerant Creator and Master of the Universe, the Son of God? This concept remains difficult to understand now as then. What if they capitulated under the pressure of the many questions others asked about their sanity? Certainly they were accused of irresponsibility as they pursued this "lost" cause as perceived by the ordinary mind and eye. Thank God for their strength and their invaluable legacy to us! But ponder the personal cost in sufferings and difficulties and terrible deaths they experienced.

Think of the Apostle Paul. His conversion precipitated him into the most profoundly joyful relationship of his life. But consider the pain, the suffering, the persecution and trials that he sustained in the process of fighting "the fight" and running "the race." He was beaten, stoned, shipwrecked, imprisoned, and faced death on multiply occasions before losing his head on the Apian Way.

Counterbalance those events with the fact that he counted everything dung except for what he had done in the name of and for the glory of his Savior. He found satisfying peace and joy, and the love he told us about. He could never be separated from the love that would not let him, and will not let us, go!

Remember Stephen, who gave his life in martyrdom, but was received personally by Christ into Glory.

Assess the lives of specific missionaries who have paid the ultimate price for their services to Christ even during our lifetime. Three men missionaries were killed in Columbia, South America a few years ago. Three men were martyred by the Auca Indians back in the 1950s. More recently Martin Burnham died in the Philippines. Consider the price early missionaries to India, China, and Africa paid. They gave up wealth, status, family and health in order to present the Gospel in distant lands. Their sacrificial service brought hope to tribes, countries and nations where vital portions of the universal Church now reside.

Envision the world wide Church community and see the oppressed, the persecuted, the threatened. See the consequences of their faith.

The burning question is: Do we want to be well? **Wellness is a choice.** First, it is a choice **to believe** but along with the authentic belief will come a choice **to experience change**. Are we willing to experience a genuine inner change that will manifest itself outwardly? Are we willing to accept exhortation and admonishment to live lives of Holiness? But the change is a work of God for our good. Will my humanistic thinking be converted to the mind of Christ? Will I become a servant? Will

I really bear another's burden? Will my pride and arrogance and selfishness be crucified daily on the cross of humility? Will I forgive and no longer carry grudges? Will I be able to turn the other cheek and go the extra mile with those that mistreat me? Will I love my neighbor as myself with agape love? Will I sincerely pray "not my will but thine be done?" Will I be grateful and content in my circumstances? Will I seek first the Kingdom? Will I give up my fear, bitterness, anger? Will I be willing to rely on God's power and not my own strength and pride? Will I step out of the quiet, secure shadows of my comfort zone and be a light for Christ in a darkened world? Will I stand up for justice, family values and against immorality in a demoralized, dehumanized society? Will I be the salt which preserves a Christian ethic and values every life because God does?

There are consequences of our choices—even for Christ!

In the incident of the healed invalid there were consequences for Christ. The authorities persecuted Christ because He healed this man. The religious leaders chose to ignore the good works but condemned Christ on a technicality. He had healed on a Sunday. This was considered "work" and against the law. Truly this seems a twisted, unbelievable interpretation of the law when we consider how much a life had been changed! The obvious spiritual application is that Christ suffered to give us healing. He suffered the persecution of the cross and the awful shame of being the sin bearer for all the world's sin. This perfect spirit carried to the grave all imperfections of all peoples that ever did or would live . There would be no remembrance of sin for whoever accepted Him as the Healer. Consideration to the alternatives and consequences for us if he had not died should incite great gratitude in our hearts. Is that gratitude sincere enough in our daily lives so that we honor and please Him in attitude and deed?

Because of Him, we possess a better life, one in which all things, both understood and mysterious, work to our good. We have obtained a life with the fullest of potentials. We can enjoy a life of freedom, unshackled, unfettered, unbound from sin, self, and the dominion of Satan.

We will choose whether to bring honor to Christ's name or whether we live lives that discredit Him and His community, the Christian Church.

It can be perturbing to have someone else summarize succinctly and eloquently what one has been mulling over and unsuccessfully trying to express. Max Lucado has said it very well on the cover of his book titled "Just Like Jesus." He introduces his book title this way:

"God loves you the way you are, but He refuses to leave you that way. He wants you to be **just like Jesus**."

That really is the point of it all! He wanted that of the Disciples, the Apostle Paul, Nicodemus, the woman at the well, and this poor paralytic…and us!

He wants us to be "well" and in a relationship with God. He waits to wrap up our sinful wounds, pour the healing wine of love and forgiveness deep within our souls and then lift us up in His powerful arms that tightly hold us to His breast and transmit His life into us.

The Apostle Paul teaches "I am crucified with Christ nevertheless I live, yet not I, but Christ lives in me. The life I live in this body I live by faith in the Son of God who loved me and gave Himself for me." (Gal 4)

In order to be well we will require a transplant. Our hearts and characters are diseased. We need the heart and mind of

Christ transplanted into us. For us to live, the indwelling life of Christ must pump through out our very beings. The natural body tries to reject that which is foreign to it. Our Adamic nature, our natural self, attempts to reject this Christ-likeness transplant. Self arrogantly justifies and rationalizes that we are not sick and morally fallen and do not need God's salvation and new life. We believe we are good, upright, moral and deserving of God's Heaven because of our own wholesomeness. In truth, our own attempts at morality and civility are "good" but fall short of God's standard and glory.

Do we want to be well? Then we must embrace the healing Savior's offer for wholeness, acquaint ourselves with His Heart and Mind which is determined in His Word, and willingly submit to the newness of eternal and abundant life by seeking His face and Kingdom, not the things of self and this earth.

The invalid recognized his need and accepted Christ's offer to be well. Our choice is clearly the same. We may listen to Christ or turn away and look for healing and answers elsewhere. He listened to Christ. We have a deep spiritual need that requires a response to the Savior's sufficient offer for healing and wholeness. We will never know His presence in our lives or the fulfillment of his promises of peace and joy unless we ponder and respond to His question.

"Will you be well?"

Chapter 3
Caleb, a Great Leader
(Listening with a Believing Heart)

While on a recent hike to Western Head in Cutler, Maine, I paused to sit and watch waves from the open ocean crash against the rocks at my feet. A literal ocean of waves seemed intent on going somewhere. Pushed and pulled by unseen winds and gravitational forces they rushed to break upon on the island cliffs and loudly shatter on the mainland shores. As far as the eye could see they pushed forward in regular repetitive rows down the coast toward Ingalls' Island and the Point of Maine. Feeling an odd sense of connection with this phenomenon, I was reminded of generations that have risen out of history, the matrix of the past, and have monotonously advanced until with a final rush to the edge of their time they frothed out. Each human wave closely has replicated the preceding generation and then receded back into the ocean of human experience.

The Christian experience is similar. Generations of Christendom have attempted to maintain a focused forward movement through the centuries of its story hoping to impart energy and assistance to the succeeding generations and to maintain strength, vitality and momentum during its run in time. The Holy Spirit, the Word of God, and the fellowship of the Saints are the unseen vital ingredients of Christian life. But

God has often used specific men and women as major influences and examples for us to contemplate.

One of the most focused men in Scripture had to have been Caleb.

Do you remember his story? In capsule form—He was previously unknown to us until Numbers 13:6. He was a leader of Judah apparently known by and picked by Moses as one of twelve to spy out the "Promised Land." He and Joshua were the only two men who returned from Canaan with optimism and the belief that God would guide them to conquer that fertile land. The other spies admitted to having viewed a beautiful land with marvelous fruits, but paralyzing fear of Giants in the land overwhelmed them. They only envisioned trouble ahead.

As a result, the Israelites listened to their fears and had complete heart failure. They cried, were afraid, and failed to do as God had ordered. Because of their disobedience, God prevented that generation of Israelites from entering the "Promised Land" except for the two men, Joshua and Caleb. That generation failed God and each other miserably and barely produced a splish-splash on the shore of their lives.

Because of Caleb's faith and courage, God promised him the foothills of Hebron for his possession and for an inheritance to pass on to his family. Forty-five years later Caleb claimed that promise! But he did not receive a gift-wrapped present from God. Despite that long interval of years, the land was unchanged. It was fertile and beautiful but the giants were still there! At eighty-five years of age, he had to earn his inheritance. He had to wage battle after battle in dependence on God. His testimony was that he still had the energy, the vigor, and the same desire for God's promised land that he had had those many years before.

Caleb was a very interesting and distinctive person. He was apparently 40-years-old when picked to be a spy for Israel. The

Scriptures, and actually God Himself, speak of him as a man "with a different spirit." (Numbers 14:24) He did not espouse the Israelite party line. The Israelites proved themselves to be fickle, unreliable people in their relationship with God. They had short attention spans. They would not focus on God and the miraculous events He had orchestrated for them. They had no substantive or enduring Faith in their Savior.

By the millions they had crossed the Red Sea on dry ground and had literally viewed the destruction of the Egyptian army by the hand of God. But they were superstitious and fearful and did not seem to understand God's character. They had no reality of God in their lives, personally or corporately. God's person and His position were ignored, underestimated, disbelieved, misunderstood, and disobeyed. They were described as stiff necked or in other words arrogant, unthankful people with no remembrance or recognition of God's mercies.

In fairness, we all lack understanding of God's awesomeness. However, it is remarkable that all creation worships God. Scripture tells us that the Heavens declare His glory (Psalm 19:1) and Nature leaves man without an excuse for ignoring God. (Rom 1:20)

All creation is paying for man's disobedience and groans to be relieved of its fallen state. But there is music in the universe. The Scriptures tell us that at the moment of creation the stars sang and the angels shouted! (Job 38:7)

Recently a science article in the *Bangor Daily News* reported that somewhere in the vastness of the universe, sound is being emitted from a black hole millions of light years away. This sound is fifty-four octaves below middle C! Humans, who have a narrow range of hearing pitches, are incapable of perceiving such a low range of sound.

One could imagine that there is a musical choir, a heavenly orchestra, out there in the heavens. Is this black hole part of the base section? Are there meteors whistling tenor and stars singing high soprano?

God is a great and awesome God. We tend to marginalize Him rather than to magnify Him. He is often only in the periphery of our minds and lives. Even if we as His creatures don't know Him as God Almighty, Creator and Sustainer of the Universe, the rest of His creation recognizes and testifies of Him daily.

No single person in man's history has been more driven or more focused to do the will of God than the Lord Jesus. And He pursued that divine will with joy because of the promise and knowledge of what was to follow this earthly life. When He said, "It is finished," His task was done. Although the human condition had not changed, Christ had changed the ultimate possibility for this fallen race from that of desperation to great hope. Mankind was still poor in spirit, wicked at heart, powerless, and arrogant. But Jesus had stayed focused and had done what the Father sent Him to do. He is our example, and Hebrews 12:2 asks us to fix our eyes on Him.

Our man in question, Caleb, had a totally different vision or perspective than the other Israelites. He focused on God's plan and will for Israel. Caleb's spirit was different. His footsteps had left their imprint in the dust of the promised land. He had been there, had viewed the fertile land and had tasted the exceptional fruits that God wanted to give them. Caleb desired what God desired: to see His people in a great place. Before spying out Canaan, Caleb had years of preparation for the task. He had been getting to know God and God was getting to know him. God had proved him in ways we do not know during those years leading up to his time of testing.

The Children of Israel would have chosen to return to slavery in Egypt and resume their relative creature comforts.

Caleb was motivated by Godly desires and was willing to endure temporary hardships. Possibly he had heard about the experiences of Noah and Abraham and Job and knew that God kept His promises even after waiting long years for the answers.

Caleb definitely had seen the Mighty God working in the great Exodus. He had been at the Red Sea. He had eaten manna from heaven. He had viewed God's spectacular activity at Mt. Sinai and had heard God speak the ten commandments. He had actually seen God's writing on tablets of stone. He had pondered and knew the power of the first commandment. Caleb had seen the ruination of those who disobeyed this Mighty God who acted justly in Holy Anger. He loved the Lord God with his heart, soul and mind and strength. Caleb had made God his God. He believed Him to be Able to do what He said. Such confidence in the Holy, Almighty One empowered Caleb with the courage and strength to be different. His mind, flooded with the vision, promises, and commands of God; and his heart overflowed with a desire to be God's servant. He dreamed of definite victory over the Giants in that dangerous land of God's largess. He knew the key to victory was his obedience. God would be responsible for the victory.

He must have experienced frustration, disappointment, and perhaps discouragement, but probably not for long, because we are told that he served God wholeheartedly. He believed unreservedly that in God's time Hebron would be his.

Where were the other leaders who had climbed Sinai and had seen God? What had happen to their memory and vision of God? Somewhere there had to have been a disconnect between their vision and their hearts because these men are hardly a footnote in history.

When his generation was gone, Caleb, then an old man, put on his armor; and with the youthful enthusiasm and energy that he had had forty five years before (Joshua 14:10), he prepared to take the Hebron hill country that God had already given him. Doubt was not a word in his spiritual dictionary. He did not flinch at the humanly insurmountable task ahead but considered it done in the eyes of God.

Caleb was steadfast, diligent, vigorous, and devoted. He was not hampered by the boundaries of humanistic thinking. God's unlimited power and possibilities were wired into his thinking. Oswald Chambers says "God gives a vision of the truth. It is not a question of what He will do, but of what we do." (in "Our Utmost For His Highest," July 8) Caleb knew what to do. He acted on God's truth that he and the Israelites were to go in and possess the land. He was not the least bit intimidated by the future because He knew the God of the future.

There would be war ahead. The giants still needed to be faced. Caleb's strength was not energized by self-righteousness but by faith in the power and presence of God. A man of deep conviction, he chose the unpopular course of believing God.

He was no slacker. He did not expect God to hand him the city keys to Hebron but expected God to use him to defeat the enemy and honor God in the process.

Joshua later would stand before the new generation of Israelites and exhort them to "Choose this day whom you will serve." Caleb had chosen early in his life. He finished life strong, focused on doing God's will for his time and country.

Because he believed and was faithful, Caleb was blessed, not only with the Hebron foothills, but also with a Godly, courageous warrior son-in-law who became the first judge of Israel. And he was able to fulfill God's promise of family inheritance by leaving his daughter the legacy of the "upper and lower springs" of Hebron. These springs apparently continue to water the fertile lands of Hebron today.

Caleb's life stands as a tribute to the Godly life and remains a model for us today. He lived his life for the purposes of God. His mind was filled with the voice and vision of God. He had a spirit submitted to the will of God.

His place, the hill country called Hebron, was part of Canaan, the Land of Milk and Honey. But God's call was not a call to retirement. Hebron was not a retirement village with great cuisine and hiking trails! Following God into Canaan was similar to being called into God's kingdom. It is not a life of filling scrapbooks with good memories. It is a life full of vitality, energy, vision, and service. It is not just an easy, happy go lucky existence.

It is a race.

It is a battle.

It is the battle of good and evil, a battle of our inner, corrupted natures competing with reborn spirits which desire Holiness, a battle of selfish tendencies attempting to subdue submissive spirits serving in the King's army.

The dreaded giants in our lives rob us of territory promised by the Savior and the Spirit of God. We are promised peaceful places and rest filled pastures, adventurous trails of faith that lead us to revelations of God on mountain vistas, fertile valleys of belief and service, and refreshing cups of water from the Spring of Living water.

Our Great God has promised us victory over giants that block our path through the promised foothills of His Kingdom. Conflict is intense and relentless.

The prideful giants of ignorance and misinformation demean and taunt the promise of forgiveness but are **overpowered** by the Revelation of God and a Spirit of repentance.

The daunting giants of fear, failure, and anxiety attack the promise of joy and peace but are **subdued** by the soothing presence of Christ.

The giants of laziness and distractions that deafen, blind, and cause general spiritual feebleness obstruct the promise of knowledge and are **defeated** by the sweat of disciplined minds enlightened by the principles and teachings of the Word of God.

The powerful giants of insubordinate spirits trample the promise of doing the work and will of God and are **slain** only by a prayerful heart, obedient to the call of Christ to be, to do, and to go...

The overwhelming giants of failures and disbelief beat down the promise of assurance but are **smitten** by the knowledge of God's wonderful sustaining love that will not let us go.

There is much work and fighting to do. There is the labor of asking and seeking, the diligence of being salt and light, and the work of Evangelizing with the Good News. But self relentlessly opposes a developing conformity to Christ's character.

Canaan is our possession by faith but is populated with giants. Victory is assured. We must not lose our focus. Even as Caleb, our minds and spirits are to be different, renewed and believing. Obedience to God's commands will get us there.

Losing focus is easy. There are numerous distractions. Sometimes we can fight a good fight or play a good game but miss the mark. As a high school freshman, I "tried out" for the freshman basketball team. At that time my school did not have a gym, so we practiced at the local college gym. As a result, there was not enough space to accommodate all the potential NBA players on the team. Some students were eliminated after a series of tryouts. I thought that I played reasonably well and showed a definite skill. The night the team was to be picked, we had a scrimmage. I did a superb job. I dribbled, weaved, intercepted the ball, made a mad dash the length of the court, outdistanced my opponents, and made a basket. My exhilaration and self congratulations did not last long. The coach blew his whistle in my face, drew the team around and with a rather ungentle demeanor asked me what was wrong with me. He informed me that I had made a basket on the wrong end and had given my opponents two points. Embarrassing indeed! Needless to say, I did not make the team. I had lost my focus. I had lost sight of the correct goal and sadly did not qualify.

Nearly a year ago now, a patient came to my office and it was soon obvious that she was experiencing depression and anxiety. With some probing it was quite apparent she felt she was losing her faith. She was upset, fearful, and tearful. Her formal faith was Catholicism. This occurred during the height of the sex scandal publicity involving the Catholic Church. We discussed faith in Christ as the sole object of true belief and that He, not people, should be the true focus of faith. She had a firm belief in Him and salvation through Him. She seemed encouraged. When I recently saw her again, she felt less depressed with some therapeutic approaches, but she was no longer involved closely with her Church. I sensed her faith continued to falter. This patient had the wrong focus. People will always fail us. There is One who will not. That, of course, is the Lord Jesus Christ.

Losing focus can seriously affect outcomes in our lives and even the ultimate outcome of our lives as was true for Caleb and the Israelites. Our eternal destiny may be at stake. For instance, living a good, moral life under the impression that that is what

God wants from us will not count for baskets or gain points in God's plan. Recognition of our own inadequacy and repentance from our arrogant sinfulness and acceptance of His gracious provision for salvation through Christ alone will gain us the goals of Fellowship with God and the Hope of eternity with Him. Humanly speaking we may play a good game but miss the mark.

In order for the Church to accomplish its God ordained goals, the Church needs to recognize God's plan. Our aims should be His aims. We need a clear vision in order to impact the next generation. Our vision should be His vision.

In the Book of Revelations, Christ addressed seven churches, which most likely represent different church ages, and commended some for their activities. He praised different churches for different reasons:

> for their patience,
> for not tolerating evil,
> for holding fast His name,
> for charity,
> for good works,
> for service, and
> for faith.

But Christ also severely condemned them for their spiritual faults and deficiencies:

> One had lost its first love of Christ.
> Some had failed to keep out evil.
> Some did not keep them selves pure.
> One was materially wealthy but spiritually poor.
> One was lukewarm toward the things of God.

The problems are palpably clear. The Christian faith is not a religion of works but a relationship with Christ, the Great Lover of the Church. These churches had not nurtured that relationship. Their works had merit but were motivated by self and not out of a deep love for the Savior.

The principle of the first commandment is inescapable when we think of focus and goals. There is no finer personal goal than that of experiencing the ten commandments as expressed by the Lord
Jesus Christ. Love the Lord God with heart, mind and strength and our neighbor as ourselves.

This is **the** principle for happy, wholesome, Holy living. If we love the Lord Jesus in **that way,** then we will have understood worship because our lives will revolve and evolve around Him and His purposes. We will have a sense of who He is and what He has done. Our Lives as a living Church should be the same. We are not talking about a moral code legislated by the church or by a religion but a desire born in lives deeply centered on the Lord Jesus and empowered by the Indwelling Holy Spirit. Lives living deed by deed, day by day, for His purposes **because we love Him.**

God's plan has at least two components. These artificially separated ideas flow into each other in the concept of Salvation.

First, Christ is not willing that any should perish but wants all to come to repentance. Salvation was His primary earthly goal for humanity. Christ came to seek and to save those that are lost. Salvation is an activity of God. He has accomplished the only means of Salvation for us. But it is something we must choose to accept or believe. As a Church we are involved. We are commanded to "go" to our families, neighbors, towns and beyond. Our life style, our prayer life, our giving of time, talents and finances will reflect our love for God and community. We must faithfully present the Good News that Christ died, was buried and rose again the third day. Evangelism is one of the duties of the Church. We need to be obedient to the Great Commission.

The response to the message will be a transaction between God the Holy Spirit and the individual whose heart listens. Christ will build His Church. We need not be anxious about that. Lift Him up, and all men will be drawn to Him.

The second desire Christ has for His Church is what He, as God, wanted for His Old Testament Chosen Tribe. Christ died for holiness, and He wants a special holy people to represent Him. We are His presence and spokespersons in a barbarian world. Peter informs us that "Jesus Christ gave himself for us to redeem us from all wickedness and to purify for Himself a people that are His very own... eager to do what is good." (1 Peter 2:14) **Note that he died to save us from wickedness, to purify us for a special people, and to be people eager to do good.** Clearly we are not saved for self realization but to have a realization of Christ in us so that the world will know that Christ is vital and real and contemporary to our individual and societal needs.

We just don't get it ! Life really isn't just about us! If it were, we would have to agree with King Solomon that "all is vanity" (Ecclesiastes), or with T.S. Eliot who speaks of life ending with not a "BANG" but a "whimper" ('The Hollow Men"), or with Shakespeare's *MacBeth* who condemns life as "a tale told by an idiot, full of sound and fury, signifying nothing." (*Macbeth*) The point is that Christ desires to live through us and will empower us to live such a life if we submit our will within His. Someone has said that the great act of worship is just that: submitting ones will to the will of God. Submission is essentially accomplished in the acceptance of God's Salvation and the willingness to pursue Holiness.

We need to turn our telescopes retrospectively, peer through the ages of History, and call out to the most important Person in this or any other universe, "God what are you doing?" As we listen and reflect as that question echoes back through time, we will hear the reassuring answer clearly, "I love you. I love you with an everlasting love. I loved you before the world began. Even before the foundations of the world, I saw and made provision for your need. I loved you with a perfect creation. I loved, sustained, and did not desert or annihilate you after that original, terrible disobedience and fall from my Grace. I loved and preserved you in the Great flood and promised you times and seasons as long as History would last. I loved you enough to reveal my awesome Holiness on Mt. Sinai where I spoke to you and wrote the Moral Code on stone tablets with **My** finger." These enduring principles convey the means for happiness in a sinful society. "I cried out with an unlimited love at Calvary. I loved you in the amazing miracle of the Resurrection. I loved you with the intimacy of my indwelling Spirit to comfort and guide and teach you. I loved you with my Letter of Love that you hold in your hand this day. My love for you is so great that your death is precious to me because you will be with me forever. I love you and am preparing a place for you where I will fellowship with you in perfect love. I am for you. Who can stand against Me?

"But through My History I have shown you that you are in a great Battle against evil. This is a battle for your souls. You must choose on which side you will fight. **You must choose me to live. Otherwise, you choose death.** I told the Israelites before they entered Canaan, 'This day I call heaven and earth as witnesses against you that I have set before you life and death, blessing and cursing. Now chose life that you and your children might live. Love the Lord your God, Listen to Him, Hold fast to Him." (Deut. 30:19-20)

Building the Church is not our responsibility. Christ will do that. We are to be His bride and His building. Saving the world is not our mandate. Christ will do that. We are His ambassadors bringing the Good News. Holiness is our endeavor. Christ will empower us. We need to submit all aspects our lives to Him as acts of worship. Our lives are to be living sacrifices Holy unto Him. (Rom 12:1)

To accomplish these two goals of Evangelism and Maturation as a Holy People, the Church must be firmly grounded in the Truth and Promises of the Scriptures. There must be Godly discerning teachers and leaders who will not listen to other voices and will not desert the faithful teaching of the Word of God. The realization of God's power will come through the faithful fervent prayers and the Holy lives of His people. The Church must hold in utmost priority the importance of serving each other, esteeming each other highly, and recognizing that love displayed in the Body of Christ is the highest recommendation of Christ to a needy world.

We need to examine ourselves. Do we have the believing mind of Caleb in a wilderness devoid of Spiritual thinking? Are we people of a different Spirit? Have we accepted ourselves in the light of God's revelation: that we are sinners by nature and that we must choose salvation? There is no middle ground. There is no place for indecision. Either we believe or we don't. Either we are faithful or we are not. Indecision is either atheism or apathy. Neither condition is acceptable to God.

Are we in the world but not of the world? The Christian's thoughts and actions should be motivated by a vision of God and His power. We must not be captivated and sidetracked by the things of this world. We need to relate all aspects of our lives to God and not marginalize Him.

Are we patiently living in Canaan and allowing the Holy Spirit to produce the fruits of love, joy, and Peace in us?

Is our service to God done wholeheartedly out of love for Him?

Caleb left a legacy of power and hope to subsequent generations. The "upper and lower springs" of living water should be pouring through us so that the landscape of our children's lives will be fertile for God. These are not waters and rivers of ourselves and our accomplishments but are the refreshing attributes of Christ and His life. If the next generation believes, then the wonders of the Christ-filled life will flow into subsequent generations. (John 7:38)

Ultimately, we should desire to be the over comers mentioned in the Book of the Revelations. Christ commended several of the seven Churches for their works but also had severe words of reprimand for their major spiritual failure. They had not remained focused on their relationship with Christ. Those who did remain strong in their love for Christ were encouraged with promises about the Final Land of Promise.

Christ is the ultimate overcomer. (Rev 3:21) He understands life's struggles because He was tempted in all the areas in which we suffer and are tempted. This fact makes His rewards and Promises more special. He promises that overcomers
will be given a crown of life,
will walk in white- because they will be worthy,
will eat of the tree of life,
will not suffer the hurt of second death,
will be given a white stone with a new name written in it,
will be given power over the nations,
will have Christ confess their name before the Father,
will have Him write His Name in them, and
will sit with Christ on the Throne.

We are going to have a new name. We were first called Christians at Antioch. What do you suppose our name will be in the New Jerusalem?

We will wear new clothes.

We will reside at a new address. (Not because of new 911 designations.)

We will live in a new neighborhood with new neighbors whose lives have been consumed with upholding the honor and glory of God.

Our task is daunting. Our goal is to know and love the Lord God of the Universe with all our substance. We may have to face personal and corporate spiritual giants, cultural giants, and generational giants. We may need to reevaluate our traditions and our humanistic rules. We need to understand that the next generation's Church's exterior may be unlike ours. The larger issue is one of the heart. The authentic future Church's interior has to be populated with those whose hearts have a relationship with Christ and a desire for Holiness in their lives. This will be the true Church.

We need to stay strong and unified around the Truth. Our Ministry is but for a brief time. Let God do the work. He will provide the energy.

He admonishes us to hold fast, be strong and watch.

Our strength will be in belief and obedience.

May our generation not fizzle and slosh against time's limits but crest and crash with an impact.

May the next generation even now be sensing the surge that will take it faithfully to its destination.

May we have the vigor of Caleb, the focus of Christ, and be faithful and true to the One who is Faithful and True.

He is calling to us! Listen to Him with a heart of a different spirit, a believing heart filled with desire to hear His voice.

Chapter 4
Trekking God's Mountains
(Listening for His Voice in the Long Silences)

Some months ago our Pastor taught several lessons from Heb 11, which is commonly known as the Faith chapter. When he spoke about Abraham, a phrase from Genesis kept ringing in my brain. God spoke to Abraham and revealed that He had a special place where He wanted Abraham to go. Genesis 22:3 explains that ABRAHAM SET OUT FOR THE PLACE THAT GOD HAD TOLD HIM ABOUT. By verse 22:9 he and Isaac had reached that place. The phrase "the places we will go" rang repeatedly through my mind until I realized it was a familiar phrase from a Dr. Seuss book, a story, I believe, Dr. Seuss had written for a graduating class at Harvard. He encouraged the class that because of their intellect and choices, they could go wherever desired.

Indeed, it is true that we can go the places we choose. We plan, work hard, establish careers, conquer professional and business goals, and travel the planet. Wisely, we organize our lives to attain future goals. God desires to use all these proper and good goals and events in His plan for us. But are these the places that God wants us to go or the places He wishes to show us?

We may choose places that are not God's choice for us. The Israelites found that place. After the spies returned from their reconnoiter in Canaan and reported that the Promised Land of milk and honey was populated by *giants*, the Israelites refused to enter the Place of God's promise.

Elijah also found that lonely spot away from God. After God had miraculously demonstrated His power on Mt. Carmel, Elijah lost his

56

trust and became afraid, depressed and alone. God found him and asked, "Why are you here?"

God's "places" are more likely to be spiritual than physical. His concern is the journey of the mind and heart, the places of Faith and Belief. God has set definite goals for His children. We are to know Him and appreciate Him and His good will and blessings toward us. Our characters are to conform to the purity of His own character which Jesus Christ demonstrated.

Oddly, God is the most misunderstood of all Bible characters. His very own people did not recognize, hear, or see Him. They underestimated, forgot, and disobeyed Him, gave Him no consideration, and doubted Him despite the fact that He is Sovereign Creator, omniscient, omnipotent, and all loving. He has given clear direction. Our path is not obscured. It is illuminated by His Word. Our goals are evident but the journey is difficult. Consider the teachings of the Beatitudes. (Matthew 5) To accomplish this life suggested by Christ requires God's enablement.

We have to listen to Him.

Our personal paths vary, but the life lessons God teaches us are the same. The joy of experiencing Him may come with difficulty and be at the end of rugged and difficult terrain because our natural tendency is to avoid God and satisfy ourselves. This journey of the heart with God has personal consequences including:

- Bearing the cross of self denial daily,
- Leaving or forsaking all to follow Him,
- Seeking the Kingdom of God first above all other desires,
- Recognizing and submitting to the Source of all that is Good and Holy, and

• Asking for and accepting His will—not our own.

These are all difficult concepts for a proud, rebellious human mind that prefers the delusion of self-righteousness and self worth rather than coming to terms with its true identity and need. The selfish, arrogant hearts of Adams' race find the Journey to God a rigorous course. Although, we may never move geographically, we will cross many rivers and valleys walking through and working out our Salvation. Trudging Life's paths, we often only faintly glimpse God and catch glimmers of places and plans we know He has for us.

His all inclusive plan for us began in eternity past. Indeed, this plan is for all. But men's fallen hearts impede belief and recognition of God's authority and blunt enthusiasm, vigor, and dedication to the only hope for mankind. God's plan is that whosoever chooses to accept His offer of forgiveness will travel the path of faith with Him. It is up to the individual. Yes, it does involve predestination and foreknowledge, but it does not exclude the free will of man. Man may or may not choose the path of God.

Have you sensed God working in your life. Is He directing you to some place of maturity and peace and joy. Are you "Trekking the mountain trails of Faith with God?"

Mountains may be places of great adventure. Climbing them tests endurance and courage. Personal stress and danger lurk amidst lofty views and magnificent beauty. The climb of faith is arduous and treacherous but the summit will reveal what we have never seen before, a fuller perspective of the Transcendent God.

We all have personal mountains. It may be that we refuse to view ourselves as God sees us, sinful and unworthy. We have insecurities and personal demons that defeat us. We have spiritual flaws and weaknesses. We are arrogant and unrepentant. Laziness and callousness interfere with our spiritual growth.

Life lessons are more about ourselves than life. Sometimes we are confused. We cannot see the whole view. Much of our journey is below the tree line. Roots and boulders block our progress. Our spiritual joints and muscles ache and weaken. We stumble, sprain and fall. Our bones splinter. Progress is slow. We are bruised and hurting, misunderstood, discouraged and let down. Like John the Baptist we question our Guide's authenticity. We are vulnerable in our exhaustion and weaknesses. We do not understand.

The mist ahead obscures our destination and our Guide. We have no concept of God's timing for us. We need to be patient, to develop reliance and trust. Otherwise our relationship with God and Christ lacks vitality. The fact that we are not alone on this journey is reassuring. Others have gone ahead. Hebrews 11 confirms that a cloud of witnesses testifies that the sometimes treacherous walk of Faith is passable and ultimately victorious. Scripture is filled with men and women who boldly and sometimes falteringly climbed their lives of Faith in God. The Spirit of God has shared their lives as examples so we can understand and learn about the One who loves and walks with us.

David walked the path of moral failure and found a forgiving God who considered him the apple of His eye.

Job traveled a way filled with great loss and suffering but found a patient and enduring God who believed in him.

Moses trudged from insecurity to great leadership and humility. He saw the God of Holiness and Glory.

Abraham stumbled along his way to great Faith and Trust and saw the God who met his needs.

Joshua and Caleb fought against peer pressure and chose the course of faith and obedience and saw the God of promise and victory.

Hezekiah knew the lonely trail of powerlessness and saw the God of Strength and Answered Prayer.

Saul (the Apostle Paul) raced his course with steadfastness even in discouragement and opposition because He knew the great God of his Salvation.

Others have shown us the importance of tears, loneliness, and pain as they explored the depths of Faith. We can not know the sweeter walk without the bitter taste of trials or sense great love and acceptance until we know insecurity and neglect. We will never experience the extent of joy and Perfect Peace (Isaiah 26:3) until we know the hollowness of life that lacks security and offers only transitory "things."

The Christian life is composed of many paradoxes.

We die in order to live.

We endure in order to reign.

We are disciplined because we are loved as children are loved by their parents.

We experience small segments of time called life. Our physical beings are trapped by a beginning called conception and an ending called death, but yet we are promised eternal life.

History writes all human experience and evolves generation by generation but one day will fold its covers and will cease to continue. But God is not confined by even the boundaries of eternity past and eternity future. If we choose, we may travel with Him to places prior to creation and places after earth's dissolution.

Turn about. Focus on the dawn of our heritage. Peer through time's misty mystery at that distant horizon. See the pinnacles, summits, and mountains preserved by Hebrew history. Our spiritual ancestors struggled up these peaks, scanned the future and wondered where God was leading them. Why a struggle? Because these places are places of self revelation and where He reveals His faithful, loving, Holy character to us and where His greatness becomes so implanted on our minds that we unhesitantly travel life with Him and seek the places He wants to take us.

Think of Mt. Ararat, Mt. Sinai, Mt. Carmel, Mt. of Olives, Mt. of Transfiguration, Mt. Moriah, Mt. Calvary! The Ancient of Days leads us to lofty heights in the Judeo-Christian Faith and tradition. In those mountains He unfolds Who He is and what He desires for His created creatures. Persons such as Noah, Moses, and the Lord Jesus guide us through life journeys that endeavor to overcome limiting boundaries in order to experience the Sovereign God.

Long ago, before the earth had experienced rain, mankind's behavior so disgusted God that He could no longer tolerate their selfish, godless ways. He chose five hundred year old Noah to be His example and messenger to that doomed generation. The Scriptures do not tell us much about Noah's experience with God prior to God's choosing him to build the ark. Noah probably had had a long learning experience with God. He was five hundred years old when God spoke of Him as being righteous. Hebrews 11:7 speaks of Noah's Holy fear and that he was an heir to righteousness. Noah held the same status in the pre law age as a Christian holds in this age of Grace. We, too, are heirs of God and joint heir with Christ. God Himself states that Job, Noah, and Daniel were saved by their righteousness. (Ezekiel 14:14,20) This righteousness stemmed from their belief, faith, trust, not their works.

Noah had an incredible, unimaginable, stabile faith and trust in God. Noah's walk through the one hundred years after God called him to build the ark must have been very difficult. There were "dry decades" of scoffing, scorn and misunderstanding, of suffering mockery, insults, and the taunts of a godless, fearless, disobedient generation. He was probably considered a lunatic because he tried to do God's work to God's specifications. God knew how to construct a vessel that would withstand the worst storm in history. Noah believed God knew and he followed God's detailed instructions.

Linda Greenlaw wrote *The Perfect Storm* about a horrific Northeast Atlantic storm that devastated part of her swordfish fishing fleet. The story was impressive, and Hollywood made a very vivid portrayal of the severity of this storm. However, this was nothing compared with God's storm. Noah's stormy ordeal had to have been the worst in history.

Noah was steadfast to God and patiently delivered God's message to many generations. For decades his conduct was governed by believing God for things not seen. Noah's faith was the yard stick by which the rest of the world was judged and condemned. What faith! He built God's sailing vessel in an arid country and waited 100 years for the fulfillment of God's promise. Despite God's long silence, Noah's incredibly deep, abiding trust and obedience preserved all human and animal life. Importantly, he confirmed what God already knew. Righteousness by faith is possible in mankind. The rest of the world was judged for their wicked disbelief.

Noah's faith was challenged before the flood, by the flood, and even after the flood. He spent over one year in the ark awaiting God's timing when a released bird would not return to the ark because it could find a nesting spot. At six hundred and one years of age, he planted his feet surely and safely back on dry ground. The belief that God was able to do and would do what He professed He would kept Noah strong and safe and on the right track. God is able. He is able "to carry you through."

We all struggle with storms whether normal daily stresses or disasters of illnesses, losses, and suffering. Is our God faithful? Do we have an enduring trust in God? Is our God compassionate? Do we believe that we will be given no more than we are able to bear? (I Corinthians 10:13) Does our God communicate with us? Are we building an ark of safety and security by listening and obeying? Have we followed His instructions which will carry us through the torrential down pouring of testing and suffering? Is our life's ship lined with planks of trust, faith, service, worship, and thanksgiving? Are there beams of Godly decisions and relationships? Is our faith caulked tightly with the strength of prayer and meditation on the promises and knowledge of the Supreme Person who holds the universe in His control? Are there holes in the bottom and leaks in the roof because we have failed to separate ourselves to Him? Have we resorted to our own thinking and ways rather than heeding His voice of direction or His plan? Have we neglected the Only One who is able to carry us through.

As a young woman, my mother started a children's choir in her small church. I remember seeing her sew the choir robes. They were angelic white with black borders. Not a great piano player, she nevertheless played and taught young children to sing. There are two songs I remember, "Walk in Jerusalem Just Like John" and "Through the Upper Window." Despite the years, I remember a few of the words.

The storms may come but fear not
O, Noah, I am nigh
and through the upper window you'll see me standing by—

There may not have been a window in the ark, but there was a door that God sealed. God wants to protect and be close to us.

Does our spirit have that upward view of a great, ever present God who holds us secure in our journey?

Noah's trip up Mount Ararat was different from most mountain climbs. He literally floated up his mountain. Nonetheless, it was a long, arduous journey to the summit! But reward day came. That difficult battle ended with a brilliant display of the victory banner, the first rainbow, and God's revelation of Himself to Noah. When the fullness of the time came, God revealed Himself as Creator and Controller of the earth and its inhabitants, and then He made a wonderful commitment to humanity. He had done as He said He would. He had patiently waited for men to turn back to Him. They ignored Him. He loved his creation but sorrowfully passed judgment and justice with a great flood. Miraculously, He had spared His creatures in a little ark. After such terrible devastation, He made a new covenant and promised that the times and seasons would continue, that there would be seed bearing times and harvest time, summer and winter, and day and night as long as history lasted,

and that never again would earth's children be destroyed with a flood like Noah's age saw. He set a reminder to Himself in the sky, the rainbow.

That rainbow stretches across the whole length of time's journey. Even today it reminds us that God covenants with us, that He keeps His promises, that He is sovereign, and that we can trust His promises of Salvation to all who believe. It is also a dreadful but necessary reminder that sinful men perish apart from a relationship with God.

As the generations pass, Mount Moriah looms into view. After God told Abraham He had a place for Abraham to go, he trekked for three days to this mountain. As with Noah, God and

Abraham had had a long relationship prior to this momentous call from God. Abraham was over one hundred years old at that point. Many years before in Ur of the Chaldeans, he had responded to God's call to a nomadic life. God had promised him that he would be the patriarch of a large nation. Now in old age and only by the miracle of God, Abraham had been given the son of God's choosing. Remember how Abraham had committed a big mistake. God had been silent too long. Abraham had tried to do God's job for Him. His muddled mind only understood the possible, not the God of the impossible. He "helped" God fulfill His promise by having a son with Hagar. Ishmael was born. What an impossible scene that was! Abraham had to learn to trust God to implement God's plan. Anxiety, doubt, impatience, and pride confused him and delayed what God would do. Abraham had a lesson to learn first. God would provide the solutions. All Abraham needed was a believing, willing heart.

God and Abraham had many years of experience together. Prior to Ishmael, Abraham had learned lessons of honesty in Egypt where he had been deceitful because of fear and lack of trust in God. (Genesis 12) Abraham had learned about generosity and God's supply in his dealings with Lot. (Genesis 13) Later he learned of God's love and justice with Lot in Sodom and Gomorrah. (Genesis 19) He fought and won battles. (Genesis 14) He had learned that God's way is the best way. Abraham was learning about God's provision in his life. God had prepared Abraham for this moment on Mt. Moriah. When God called him there with his only son of promise, Abraham knew God, believed in God's promise, and trusted God to provide the necessary Sacrifice. Astoundingly, he raised his dagger to plunge it into the son of God's promise and the son he loved so deeply. What a terrible, long, silent moment that must

65

have been. But God in His time, at the end of man's time limit, at what seemed the last moment, met the need with the promised sacrifice.

Interestingly, Mt. Moriah became a place of sacrifice. Abraham first sacrificed there. David bought this spot and offered a sacrifice of repentance. (1 Chronicles 21:18-21,22:1) It became the site of Solomon's Temple. Atonement for the sins of the people was made there. This place became Mount Zion.

Mt. Moriah casts a long shadow across the ages to the site where God provided for all Humanity. Outside Jerusalem's walls, Christ died as an outcast from the Jewish religion. He was unwelcome in this Holy City or the Temple, a house to His Father. The keepers did not know Him. He was Jewish, worshiped in the Temple, but had no true religious affiliation. He was eschewed by orthodox religious leaders who plotted His demise. "He came unto His own but His own received Him not." In their own self-righteous, vain traditions and legalistic, prideful philosophies, they forgot they stood on the Holy historical ground of promise and provision. Blind and deaf, they could not see the Holy Son of God or heed his call. They did not recognize their need nor understand His Ministry. As He died in the shadow of their Holy Hill, they sat in robes of self-respect and in gates of legalism. Totally misunderstanding the role of God's law that had brought them to that very moment and to the Lord Jesus Christ, they had Him killed outside the city, outside the camp. He was murdered under Roman and Jewish law by organized religious activity. While smugly holding their heads high, they should have been on their knees in repentance and grief and awe before God's provision for them. The Church's foundation is not works of righteousness that we have done but the work of righteousness that He has done. The true foundation is Jesus Christ Her Lord.

As we journey on, Mount Sinai's dark peaks come into view. Just three months after leaving Egypt and experiencing Israel's salvation at the Red Sea, the children of Israel had forgotten God's goodness and protection and were so disgruntled, unhappy and ungrateful that God had a meeting with Moses on the Summit of Sinai.

God descended to the top of Mt. Sinai and called Moses up to Him. Moses was not a young man, but he climbed Mt Sinai at least six times and twice spent forty days and nights there in the presence of God.

But like Noah and Abraham, Moses did not just incidentally arrive on this scene and be chosen randomly to meet with the God of the Universe. God and Moses had had many encounters. Some were not pleasant. Moses even knew what it was to have God angry at him. There were quiet years in Moses' life. Although raised in palace luxury, he became a shepherd totally removed from the main stream of the daily life of the Israelites. But one day on Mount Horeb where Moses was tending sheep, God spoke to him from a burning bush. God and Moses had an interesting beginning. Right away Moses tried God's patience. Sometimes it seems as though Moses' trek with God was as difficult for God as it was for Moses. When God revealed Himself and His purposes to Moses, Moses sparred, questioned, and rationalized. He wanted to know who God was. God answered that He was the "I Am." Moses lacked confidence that the children of Israel would listen to him. He couldn't talk to Pharaoh because he was not eloquent. God repeatedly and patiently demonstrated His power with miracles. Moses still had trouble trusting God's ability. God got upset with him. There was one point at which God contemplated killing Moses due to a lack of obedience to God's prescribed ways and plans. (Exodus 4:24) Moses seemed proud, whiney, arrogant and disbelieving. Yet he was greatly loved by God who made him His spokesman and the greatest leader Israel would ever have. He eventually was said to be "more humble than anyone on the face of the earth." They had had a stormy relationship with intensive interactions before Mount Sinai hovered into Moses view. With God's help, Moses had dealt with Pharaoh and the plagues, executed the great Exodus, honored God at the Red Sea and intervened with God for the grumbling, fickle, unhappy, ungrateful, and unbelieving people.

Surrounding Sinai's peak, the dark, lowering clouds, the loud rumbling thunder, and bright flashes of lightening hid God's glory. Gazing upon Sinai, we suddenly recognize that the presence and sight of God would consume our sinful natures. This awesome show of power warns us of the nature of the Holy One we have been summoned to hear. These moments may be moments of either great revelation or possible massive misunderstanding. God audibly spoke the words of the Moral Law which He later wrote with laser accuracy in stone tablets with His very own finger. He gave them to Moses (Ex 33:18, 32:16). He clarified for mankind what He had already written in their Hearts, but they had buried it beneath selfish layers of uncontrolled wants. Indifference and denial could no longer be an excuse for man's ungodly, antisocial, immoral behavior. God now had said it. God had written it. He wrote it, not on a 5000-pound stone found in an Alabama court house, but in tablets of the heart and conscience. The first commandment was the most difficult because man's selfish, rebellious nature blurs our vision. Nearsighted, we worship at the altar of self. We do not worship at the altar of the Worthy One, the Creator God, Who had brought us through perilous courses but whom we can not always clearly identify.

Israel was given ten moral laws. The first was broken even before they moved camp. At the foot of Mt. Sinai, they worshiped a golden calf. To understand our imperfect and defective state, we only need the first Commandment. Possibly, God gave us ten Laws so we cannot fool ourselves about our own righteousness. We still miss the point many generations later. If we follow our unwholesome tendencies with our inadequate, weak, selfish and incomplete Adamic natures, we infringe on the rights of God and others. Christ condensed the Law very simply for us, "Love the Lord with all your heart, mind, soul— and your neighbor as yourself." Moral Law could no longer legitimately be questioned. It was established forever more.

Clearly, we fail to measure up to God's standards.

Much happened on and around Mt. Sinai. God revealed Himself to Moses and Israel to whom He spoke and wrote His moral, societal, and religious laws. Angry with the Israelites' idolatry, He responded to Moses' prayerful pleading to spare them for the sake of God's testimony to the world. He displayed His glory but protected Moses from it. God covered Moses with His hand in the cleft of the rock. Moses' radiant face reflected that glory to his people.

God's glory exposed man's sinful nature. A hierarchy of sacrifices was established to remind Israel of sinful hearts needing forgiveness. Lingering at Sinai is not comfortable, but remembering points us centuries ahead to another Mountain where the Lord Jesus shone with His Glory and was acknowledged by God the Father. Christ's brilliant transformation on the Mount of Tranfiguration may have been muted by His humanity, but was dramatic and awe inspiring. Moses, the law-giver, was present at the mountain experience. His brilliance was lost in the glory of the Grace-giver, who inspired Peter to build small tabernacles of worship.

Sinai is the place where we glimpse the awesome Holiness of God, the humanly impossible but righteous expectations of God and the revelation of our inadequacy and need for God.

Strangely, some of us might linger in our own strength and tent awhile beside Sinai. We misinterpret what God has said and live amidst the boulders of our pride, egos, self-righteousness and legalistic, pharisaical thinking. Blinded by our attempts at self radiance, we can not see God's glory and do not see the path ahead. It is the long path to the greatest act of Humility that creation would ever experience. At the end there is the faint glimmer of a cross that answers our desperate need.

We are slow to learn of God and to recognize our needy situation. We stumble over our limited intellects and incomprehension. We are caught amidst the rock slides of distractions, apathy, spiritual laziness, and unrecognized disobedience disguised as humanistic thinking. Dark clouds of denial, rebellion and inadequacy hide the glory and justice of a loving God.

We construct idols of the heart that will not confront us but will permit our self delusions. They do not fulfill us but they do not condemn us. They do not demand holiness or justice. We do not tremble or faint before them. Although driven by and devoted to them, we do not recognize their power to ruin us.

Mt. Sinai is a scary place. That experience points out all that man is **not**. Centuries later this very same God of Sinai (the I Am of the Old Testament) sat with His disciples on another mountain and lovingly taught them about Godly attitudes of the Heart. There were no darkened clouds, no crashing thunder or lightening. Christ gave nine Beatitudes. These were principles of being, not just doing. The Law alone never brought about these attitudes in mankind. He spoke of an extraordinary inner life not external behavior. Christ confirmed that the law would exist as long as the earth did. It would last throughout time. Christ revealed the underlying meaning of the Law. It showed how morally impoverished man is and the need for a supernatural inner change of Heart. Christ had come to fulfill the Law. His life exemplified all that He taught that day. He would be the unblemished final Sacrifice for sins.

From Sinai the centuries whirr by in a blur. The years cascade rapidly through the hazy mystery of the "past." Time tumbles forward through the woes and joys of Human History. Read through the Covenants God made with man. Glimpse great champions of the Faith who had a vision for the unseen and the unseeable. They believed in the Creator God and were willing to do battle beside Him. In the fullness of time, God, himself, entered into the human race for a thirty-three year, painfully difficult struggle with poverty, human temptation, personal misunderstanding and isolation. His life culminated in a "failed" ministry complete with disillusioned disciples and a ghastly death when He weakly stumbled up a hill called Golgotha to be crucified among thieves.

How could Almighty God, the source of knowledge, be so misunderstood? His own followers were unbelieving, unseeing, deaf, and so forgetful that he repeatedly had to demonstrate His power, His proof of authority over the natural, and the supernatural, and over illness and death.

The wise do not linger at the foot of Sinai or sit on its summit but follow the short cut leading to a Mount where three crosses stand silhouetted against the sky. The middle one marks the beginning trail to the foothills of the New Covenant of God with His people. Whether Calvary was an actual Mount is not clear. In tradition it is. Old hymns such as "The Old Rugged Cross" and "Up Calvary's Mountain" confirm this idea.

The important fact is that Golgotha is where God the Son, in the deepest possible humiliation, submitted His own power and authority to the will of God the Father for the sake of humanity and became the only worthy sacrifice that met the demands of the law for us. Once and for all, he died.

Mankind individually now could accept or reject the only acceptable sacrifice to and the only way to the Father.

Christ is Victor in history's greatest, longest battle which actually began prior to the Garden of Eden when Satan led his rebellion into Adams's race. Paradoxically, this war continues to the current times in each of our lives. It is a spiritual battle for our souls. The paradox is that it has been won. The sting of death is soothed and the power of sin is broken. Measured in the expanse of eternities, victory took but a moment but was anticipated by thirty three of Christ's difficult earthly years and by His bloody sweat in the Garden of Gethsemane. It was the culmination of a Ministry so special that the sun would not shine until after it was finished. But the full realization of that victorious moment is understood only by trekking three more days to gaze into an Empty tomb and hear the Angel's resonating words which have blessed generations of believers, " He is not here. He is risen.."

The "world" does not understand the battle or recognize the victory because the battlefield is confused with the sounds and smells of defeat. There are sickening taunts from those passing by, onerous jabs and mockeries of the Roman soldiers and the religious leaders, and the stench of death emanating from cynical unbelieving nay-sayers who whisper that if He were God He would do what any human would do. He would selfishly take Himself off the cross and go His own way. Understanding God and His purposes and ways is not something humans do well. God's mind is far above our comprehension. These unbelievers did not know what they were seeing. Their only true Hope was dying before them.

The smoke of misunderstandings stupefied their minds. Disbelief and sadness is heard in the soft, fearful weeping of a Mother whose good, precious and uniquely special Son is dying on the battlefield. Fear vibrates in the high pitched wailing of the daughters of Jerusalem as they watch this unbelievably righteous man hang on a criminal's cross. For some, the agony of God was too much to see. Others were fearful for themselves. There is a horrible silence in their absence. Those He had loved and in whom He invested His earthly life and ministry, His disciples, had disappeared. In earlier moments the dejected, disappointed, contrite sobs of Peter can be heard.

But the saddest, most pathetic, and haunting of all sounds is the cry of a son forsaken by His Father. Heaven was silent. The Father who had been His sustainer, His source of teaching, the One whose will He came to do and whose glory he came to show remained aloof. How painful was Christ's agonizing cry of desertion!

But hush! Hear the sounds of victory! Sense the muted joy because Jesus had completed His course. He had come to do the will of the Father. He knew the joy of what lay ahead. There was encompassing warmth of love. What greater love is there than to give oneself for another. He had made the ultimate sacrifice.

Paradise's beautiful music, not detectable to bystanders, was certainly heard by the thief who confessed belief in this Savior who died only as God could.

And the bugle of God's victory was blown by His weakened dying Son in His cry, "It is finished."

Within the dark hours of our Savior's Passion another noise can be heard! Listen! Rocks crack, boulders break, tombs gap open as the earth convulses with a deep rumble and releases the dead bodies of Holy men.

Hear that faint, distant, ripping sound. The veil in the Temple has been torn asunder. Hallelujahs and praises rise! We now have access to the Father through the Only High Priest, the Lord Jesus Christ, the Sacrifice for all men.

Sweet, brave voices testify in awe and confession. The observing Centurion exclaims, "Surely this was the Son of God!" For at least two converts, there was great singing and jubilation in Heaven even though there must have been unbelievable sadness at the Son of God's terrible earthly plight.

There was no question of why Christ was nailed to that cross. He had claimed to be God. This criminal activity was attested to by a placard written in three languages, Aramaic, Latin and Greek and tacked to His cross. It clearly stated, "This is Jesus, King of the Jews." His crime was verified by mockers who said, "He claimed to be God, so let Him get Himself down off the cross." The Centurion's positive confirmatory confession, "surely this is the Son of God," was further proof of His claim.

They knew they were killing the One who claimed to be God. They, the religious leaders, saw dimly through their own perverted religious and political cataracts. They did not believe. With the clarity of honest examination, the Centurion believed.

Matthew tells us that there were those who left that crucifixion beating their chests, sometimes a sign of victory. They believed Christ had been defeated. He no longer would be an annoyance or threat. Little did they understand. They were deluded. Behind the dark shroud of the Lord Jesus' shame and humiliation existed the bright glory of God's agape love shining around an old Roman cross and casting a lengthening shadow over centuries of Christendom. This humble symbol demonstrates the powerful love of the Father in heaven for His created beings.

74

How do we approach the Redemption "story?" What is our perspective? Are we open and believing or reserved, cynical and closed to the miracle of Salvation by the blood of the Lamb of God? Is the crucifixion truly the expression of God's love or just some weird historical event manipulated by deranged or misguided people? Is there a contemporary need for this event in our own lives and current society?

Peering back to the dawn of our faith, we have watched these Patriarchs and the Lord Jesus Christ struggle along very difficult paths. Yet they reached momentous places with God. They have led us to some first inklings and glimpses of an awesome God. Reaching out to His proud creation for eons of time, God has waged a great spiritual battle of Good versus Evil, a battle for the hearts and minds of mankind. God is the source of all that is "good and perfect." These are the things He wants for our lives in this darkened, troubled world. He wants to journey with us because He is the only good and healthy way through our chaos.

These great men, Noah, Abraham and Moses, were still walking the trails of sanctification in their old age. There was a continuum of progression in their lives in knowing, experiencing and doing the will of God. We have seen these old men striving to understand the Person and Purposes of God. They had hiked for decades in a developing relationship with God and had proved their faith prior to their fantastic Mountain experiences. Someone has said that God will test faith to confirm it, never to see if it will fail. Their personal worthiness did not afford them summit views of God. Their faith counted for righteousness and won them Mountains peaks. They had walked, and talked and had submitted and had been molded into men that God could use. Through them He would speak to not only their but future generations. Many lessons are implicit in their lives.

First, the fact that life is a warfare is either not recognized or is underestimated. Recognition that God is the most important Person in our lives is of tantamount importance in this battle. It is the first Commandment. We are to have no other gods before us. Noah's, Abraham's, and Moses' generations neglected this moral law. Ignorance and neglect drew devastation and condemnation. Our belief system and worship are of supreme importance in whether we win or lose our own personal spiritual battles.

Second, God is Sovereign over His creation. He demonstrated that many times. No stronger proof of that fact is necessary than the sequence of events of Noah and the flood. Remember God, as Controller of the Universe, has made a Covenant with earth and the people therein. He has granted us the times and seasons.

Third, God is "long suffering." He is patient with us as individuals and as His creation. Noah was six-hundred years old when God revealed His awesome power, position, and promises to Him. He saw the first rainbow and experienced God's sovereignty over all things, the earth, and they who dwell therein. Abraham, the founder of a great nation that would be God's oracle to the world, was over one-hundred years old before he fully understood God's great Provision. Moses was over eighty when he started his career as God's chosen leader of the Israelites, an intermediary between God and His people, and transcriber of the Law. Only in old age would he see God's Holiness and Glory and have his face literally reflect the glow of God.

Fourth, although patient, God will not allow sin to go on indefinitely. He defined a specific moral code that honest men realize they cannot keep. Because of our innate moral deficiency, we lack the ability to measure up to Holiness.

Mankind needs a system to express repentance and a method for God to grant forgiveness, a way for God to fulfill His desire to fellowship with His sinful Creation. Judgment fell on Noah's generation which ignored God. It fell in Abraham's generation on Sodom and Gomorrah where righteous men could not be found. It fell repeatedly on the Israelites, God's special people, because they were proud and unbelieving. God will not always tarry with the unrepentant sinner. The wages of sin is death. However—

Fifth, God has always provided a way of forgiveness. The ancient religious law given the Children of Israel prescribed a precise sacrificial system for the covering of sins. But the Sacrifice of Christ ushered in the Age of Grace where forgiveness and salvation are the free gift of God. Eternal life is a relationship with Christ not a performance to please God.

Christ's earthly course was the shortest yet perhaps the longest of these men we have mentioned. As the Ancient of Days, He Journeyed from Eternity past then walked for thirty three years in time to reveal God to us. He, too, is a spokesman. He is the literal Word of God, the literal representation of God, the incarnate God, and spoke the words of the Father. He taught that the Godly heart is not powered by works of righteousness that we have done. We do not have the moral energy or the moral standing. We need forgiveness and new life, God's indwelling life. If we are to be what He wants us to be, we must be born again, enter God's family and become his children by faith. God's law taught us that we are morally deficient, incapable of perfection and cannot stand in the presence of a Holy God. Our sins must be judged and the penalty paid.

These transactions occurred on the cross. Our journey begins in earnest when we come to this sacred place of sacrifice and kneel in repentance before the Savior. Christ, the eternal **I**

AM, the same One who declared that fact to Moses, is the only provision for the sins of us all. He bridged that great chasm of broken relationship with God so that we might walk with God, talk with Him and be molded by Him. He is our personal companion on the trek of sanctification as we falteringly climb our own Mountains of faith with Him.

Sixth, God has chosen His people to be His spokesmen. The Universal Body of Christ, the Christian Church, must face the hidden future with the Eye of Faith and with the Mind and Heart of Heaven. We are His ambassadors to all the earth in our generation. We possess and proclaim the Good News that saved us. In the past, He chose Isreal and specific individuals to reach nations and generations. We are His chosen for this time.

Seventh, this journey of the heart with God may at times be lonely, but we are never alone. He has promised never to leave us or forsake us as His disciples. Often we, ourselves, are the major reasons for the difficulty. We battle our own rebellious, unrepentant, proud natures. There may be other reasons that the life of faith is difficult. Although unaware, Job was chosen to do battle for God when Satan challenged God. But remember we are not given trials beyond that which we can bear. We will learn of His presence in our trials which purify us until we come forth as gold. (Is 43:1-2, 1 Peter 1:6-7)

Eighth, Our lives influence others to an extent we may never know on earth. Noah, Abraham, and Moses did not know that their legacies would last thousands of years, even until the end of time. Most of us will be forgotten within a generation if not within days of our deaths. These men continue to influence lives. They are examples of Godly men forced into circumstances unimaginable to them. Within those circumstances they developed spiritual maturity. The life principles they learned are still valid these many centuries later.

They listened to God. As parents, friends and associates we are planting seeds that may carry on for generations also. What will our legacy be? We are planting and reaping eternity's harvest.

Listen closely to that great cloud of witnesses that has gone before.(Heb 12:1) Persevere! Be patient! Be obedient! Let's keep our nose to the grindstone of life but our hearts lifted to the great God of Heaven. Listen to Him! He is speaking to you.

If the Silence is too long, or the distractions too great, or earthly noises too loud, or the lure of this life too strong to hear Him, **look up** at Him. In the stillness of your heart **read His lips** as they trace His Words of hope and encouragement written in the Scriptures.

Chapter 5
Opposition to the Savior
John 10
(Hear Him in the Difficult Moments)

A few days hence would be His Last Supper with His disciples, an intimate night celebrating the Passover with friends, a precious night of patient instruction and teaching before the hellish firestorm would strike and engulf Him. That night would hold the loneliness of dreadful agony in Gethsemane's Garden and would see Godly abhorrence of sin because God's perfection knew that the awful personal effects of sin would soon fall upon Him. But the night would see victory in Christ's full submission to the Father's way. It would be the night of the expected but deeply hurtful deception and traitorous betrayal and begin the long final humility that would lead Him through Pilot's courts where no fault could be found with Him. He would pass by harsh, mad demands crying for a criminal's death by crucifixion, sit through the soldiers' mockeries and curious observers' insults, and endure the silence of His friends' pathetic desertions and denials. He would struggle along the arduous, dusty road that stretched to Calvary where He would be so emotionally and physically spent that another had to carry His cross. He, the innocent God-man, would die a painful cruel death on a rugged Roman cross with spikes piercing His hands and arms, lovingly outstretched to embrace the world.

But tonight Christ is at a party in Bethany, a place where we have seen Him before, on a different occasion. Bethany was the village where Mary and Martha had entertained Christ in Martha's home and where the sisters taught us, as they will tonight, something of worship. Bethany is the place He demonstrated His supernatural power over death and proclaimed Himself to be the Resurrection and the Life by raising Lazarus from the dead.

Apparently the following Sunday He would ride upon a donkey in that triumphant entry into Jerusalem from the road that led to Bethany. The people would lay palm leaves and their cloaks along the route and shout Hosanna in gratitude and praise to Him.

Later we will meet Christ here again. After His resurrection He will lead His disciples out on the road to Bethany once more to the place that they would see His human image for a final time. Paradoxically, He will claim He will never leave or forsake them. Then, astoundingly, He will ascend into the Heavens in front of them and leave them! But the angel will come and reassure them and us that in like manner He will return at some future time.

Simon the Leper had opened His home for this special occasion. Christ must have healed this man. The likelihood of a leper throwing a party and expecting anyone to attend is highly doubtful. The only cure for leprosy in those days was healing. Undoubtedly, Christ had profoundly touched Simon's life. Perhaps Simon was representative of the group that had come to honor this Christ who had reached out and cured the blind, the lame, the sick, the lepers, and the demon possessed.

So tonight, we find Christ on a happy occasion given in His honor. Finally, He is being recognized in an intimate but semi public event for being who He is—the wonderful compassionate Son of God. Although this is a different home, He is with the friends whom He loved. Present were Mary, Martha and Lazarus, who a short time before had miraculously been restored to life after being dead for four days. Most likely Christ's disciples were in a partying mood as well because we know Judas was there. The Apostle John has recorded the celebration. Probably the house was filled with many who were indebted to Christ and wished to honor the Lord for changed lives too.

This was an incredible event. The personalities present were exceptional people. They all would go into an historical narrative to be read and studied for centuries. (Mark 14) The Central Figure of all of history was present that night. The others are historical footnotes but remain as a source of teaching for us because of there relationship to Christ.

Circulating about the room is forthright, practical Martha serving the guests. She is the one whose house Jesus visited. While Mary sat listening at Christ's feet, Martha got distracted and harried with preparations for her Guest and eventually asked Him to intervene and have Mary help her. Martha tended to be more direct and confrontational and appeared more inquisitive and less sensitive or emotional than Mary. She was the one who met Jesus and questioned Him when Lazarus died. But she loved Him and professed knowledge of His identity and belief in Him after He had proclaimed who He was to her. (John 11) Christ's response to her request teaches us about worship, "Martha, Martha.... Mary has chosen what is better." (John 10)

My sympathies are with Martha. She demonstrated her caring and love with activity. For some of us, it is easier to proclaim love and devotion by service rather than by pure expressions of worship. Unfortunately, there is a bit of self in service. We can always say, "I did this," or "I did that," for the Lord. Whereas, if we simply stop and adore the Lord for Who He is, or intently listen to what He has said, or be grateful for what He has done, worship is pure and not tainted with self and works.

Note Lazarus is reclining at the table with Jesus. We can see them conversing but are not privileged to know their conversation. Chatting with Almighty God could be intimidating? Do you suppose the Palestinian weather or politics were discussed? Or were they discussing their precarious situation and the plot to kill them. But they were friends and Lazarus had to have been grateful for his life. He is the one that the Lord loved but chose to let go through death's door and lie in a cold, desolate tomb for four days in order to show the magnificent power of God and to demonstrate who Christ is. Christ is the source of Life. He gives life. Death does not have dominion over Him. He is the Resurrection. He is our Hope. Do you suppose that Lazarus talked about where he might have been and what he might have seen during those four days in the tomb? Do we share with the Almighty God that we are grateful for the New Life we have because of His powerful personal victory over death?

Once again we find Mary at the feet of the Master. Previously in Martha's house she sat at His feet and listened. Christ commended her for worship. She was the sensitive one. When Lazarus died, she was found mourning, surrounded by concerned Jewish friends while Martha was outside confronting the Lord for not coming in time to save Lazarus. Mary also loved the Master and came quickly to Him when she knew He had arrived. She fell at His feet weeping and pouring her heart out. (John 11) When Jesus saw her great sorrow, His loving heart overflowed with compassion, and He wept.

And now, on this special night, she is at His feet again anointing them with expensive, special ointments and drying them with her hair. Her heart is bursting in gratitude to the Lord. Again her worship is accepted by the Lord. Judas is sniping in the background about wasting money on ointments that might better have been spent on the poor. Christ tells Judas to stop his gripping and to leave Mary alone. She is doing a good and honoring thing.

Also hanging around were some inquisitive party crashers who wanted to talk with Lazarus about his miracle and to see Christ who had performed it. Many came to believe in Christ after meeting Him.

Lazarus' testimony, Simon's hospitality, Martha's service, and Mary's worship were powerful forces in introducing Christ to their community. Let us all take heart and honor the Lord in ways we are able and gifted.

Over there in the background, Judas whines, snivels, and criticizes. His complaints are hypocritical. He moans that Mary's expensive perfume should have been sold and given to the poor. This is nothing more than an expression of a tremendous greed. He was a thief and was dipping into the money bag for his own purposes. He was overpowered by greed and possibly a disappointment in this future King who had been a total political and religious disaster and was not helping Judas' ambitions. Judas's defective character blinded him to the good, the beauty and the perfection in Christ's character and made him a traitor to the King of the Universe. Unlike Thomas who overcame his doubt and Peter who overcame his impulsive behavior, Judas never demonstrated a change of character or an acknowledgment of Christ as the Lord. Both

Peter and Thomas professed publicly a personal belief in Christ as the Son of God and as Lord. Their changed lives demonstrated it.

On the surface we sense a happy time, a good party with honorable people except for one. Christ should have been relaxed among His friends who desired to honor and thank Him for the miraculous things that He had shown them, done for them and taught them.

Mary 's brother had been dead and in the grave four days. She had lost hope of seeing him on this earth again. We all know how devastating, how lonely, how painful, how despairing, how emotionally overwhelming and how final death can be. But the Master Healer had raised her brother back to her. The brother that she loved so much was now living in her home again. Can you imagine the gratitude that she must have felt to Christ for this beyond remarkable feat? Yet in her act of gratitude and worship she was criticized. Tomorrow's threatening dark clouds were already gathering. An incredible sinister background was becoming evident behind this special moment of joy and adoration. These moments would soon blur into the sounds and sights of the next few days:

- the jangle of thirty pieces of silver in the money bag of the traitor,
- the tromp, tromp of soldiers coming to get Him,
- the taunts of mockers,
- the horrible cries of the crowd,
- the shadow of that middle cross of Calvary,
- the hurried burial by unlikely disciples who were not His close friends who had deserted Him in His dying moments.

The fearsome opposition was mounting and would not be stopped. Judas' complaint that night was but the tip of the iceberg. The rulers wanted Christ's life and that of Lazarus' too. Christ threatened their authority, their positions and their political status, and they wanted to be rid of Him even by murder. Christ had met extreme opposition through out His life. He must have been exhausted by all the controversy, the belittling, the downplaying and devaluating that He had undergone.

It seemed incredible that this gentle Man had generated such hatred against Himself. His life had been so humble as a carpenter's son, who until three years before seemed to have been a relative unknown. He had no *guile* in Him. He appealed to and reached out to all peoples. He spoke to all. He touched the untouchable. He loved children and the outcasts. He had no cultural, racial, or gender prejudices. He loved and helped people even to the point of the doing the miraculous. He taught wisdom and Truth.

But from our vantage point in time, we should not be surprised at this sad turn against Christ. The first century Jew had misconceptions about the Messiah. God's plans and predictions were misunderstood. The Messiah would come and be the Israel's Savior in a national sense. He would free them from the current Roman rule. He would set up His rule and reign in this world. Of course that moment would come at some point, but it is still a time we await. God's way and timing needed to be understood in the total revelation of Scripture.

Christ had unfinished business first. He would be the spiritual Savior and would bring New and everlasting life to those who would believe, Jew or gentile. He would gather an army of believers, the Church, the Saints, who would return some future day to set up His Kingdom.

That the Savior would be opposed was known prior to creation. Scripture states that He was slain before the foundation of the world. Opposition to Christ was predicted in the garden of Eden. God told the Serpent, Satan, that Satan would bruise Christ's heel but Satan's head would be crushed by woman's seed.

The hardships and troubles that the Israelites endured were due to selfishness and disobedience, but the onslaught of temptations enticing them away from God were undoubtedly concocted in the pit of Hell in the hope that God would annihilate His people and exclude the possibility of a Messiah/ Savior. Even during Christ's earthly trial, troubled Israel was under the iron hand of Roman rule. But God had miraculously preserved the lineage of David. Although Christ's parentage was even questioned during His lifetime, New Testament accounts describe both Mary's and Joseph's genetic line back to David lest there be any question about fulfilling the Messianic promises to David.

Prophetic predictions show Christ to be a Majestic King and Savior, a powerful judge. Somewhat paradoxically there are passages that describe Him as a sad, sorrowful and wounded Savior. Ponder Isaiah 52:14:

"Just as there were many who were appalled at Him His appearance was so disfigured beyond any man-his form marred beyond human likeness"

Isaiah 53 tells us that there is
No beauty or majesty that would attract us to Him, nothing in His appearance that we would desire Him.
He is Despised and rejected by men.
He was a Man of sorrows and familiar with suffering.
He was oppressed and afflicted yet He did not open His mouth.
He was cut off from the land of the living for the Transgression of His people.

He was assigned a grave with the wicked and with the rich in His death though He had done no violence nor was any deceit in His mouth.

Herod gave orders to kill all the male Jewish children in Bethlehem two years and younger around the time of Christ's birth. His explicit purpose was to murder the newborn King.

His heritage as a carpenter's son did not fit the Royal image. After all we are told that "no good thing" comes out of Nazareth.

Even His family did not understand Him. His parents misunderstood when He first went to temple and was found expounding with the Temple leaders. His half brothers did not comprehend who He was.

The Temptations in the Wilderness were a direct attempt by Satan to have Christ divest Himself of His Godly character, to ruin Him and have Him abdicate His Kingdom for worldly gain and prestige. Christ's life had been very humble to the point in time at which He was offered power and Kingdoms by the "Prince of the Power of the Air." Such an offer of wealth was truly a test.

Some opposed Him for His claims about Himself. He stated He was the Son of God and was equal to God. He held a special relationship to the Father, His Abba. He was preexistent and claimed to have lived before Abraham's time. He was from God. His teachings were from the Father. He declared Himself to be the Christ. (John 10:25, 33) These claims were incomprehensible for the disciples of Moses and the children of Abraham who awaited a National Messiah.

He was opposed for His revolutionary teaching that religious life was not about keeping the Law but was a life of the

Spirit. Life was a relationship with God not a performance to please Him.

More often than not, what He did was not as much an issue as when He did it. He was Lord of the Sabbath but was faulted for breaking the Sabbath with His good works.

He was opposed because of His behavior. He accepted worship. He cleansed the temple of money changers that defiled the purposes of the Temple. He authoritatively debated and defied the religious leaders. He pointedly and aptly stood up to their weaknesses and hypocrisy.

He was opposed by rational minds that were blinded by greed, by power, by tradition, by Legalism, by politics, by humanistic thinking, by religiosity, by hypocrisy, by disbelief. He was too lowly born. (John 6:42) Even His brothers did not believe in Him. (John 7:5) He was called "demon possessed." (John 7:20)

Incredibly, His Miracles, the Testimony of John the Baptist and of changed lives, the astonishing voice of God Himself approving of His Son, and the very Truth Himself could not overcome or even counterbalance the Master Liar, the Father of Lies (John 8:44) who deceived rational minds so that they could not think outside "the box." Hemmed in and barricaded by pride, prejudice, fear, self, and false religiosity their minds and souls were numbed and could not perceive the depths of Christ, His hard teachings and revolutionary claims.

Why did He endure so much? To be the Savior! He came to seek and save the lost. He was the perfect Lamb of God. He fulfilled the requirements of the Law for us and became the sacrifice for all peoples. He alone was mankind's Hope! Once and for all.

Why did He humble Himself?
He came to identity with us and to be our example. "Consider Him who endured such oppositions from sinful men so you will not grow weary and lose heart." (Heb 12:3) We are told in that same passage to "fix our eyes" on Jesus. He knew racial and cultural prejudices, endured poverty and hard work, suffered the misunderstanding of family and friends, suffered the hurt of the less physically attractive, felt the searing pain of desertion, was tempted and suffered in all manner such as we, yet with out sin.

Paradoxically, God humbled Himself:
From Glorious Riches to abject poverty,
From Almighty Creator to humble servant,
From powerful God to weak humanity,
From pure Heaven to a fallen, cursed earth,
From the object of angelic Adoration to the focus of human hatred and debasement,
From Giver of Life to Receiver of a cursed, shameful death,
From Source of mercy to the Brunt of men's mercilessness
From the Fountain of Love to the Cesspool of undeserved hatred
From the loving Cleanser of hearts to the Recipient of the dirty deeds of the heart
From a perfect Spirit state to the frailties of the human body.

We can know that our God understands us, our frailties, our losses, our hurts, our predicaments, whether physical or moral. Not only does He understand but He loves us, is compassionate toward us, provides for us, has shown us the path through this life but more importantly has provided the way for eternal life.

But worldly opposition continues. Paul tells us "For those that don't believe, the preaching of the cross is foolishness." ("to those that are perishing," I Corinthians 1) Why? The world does not wish to be enlightened to its imperfections and sinfulness. But the enlightening Truth of Scripture can not be denied. The Truth is, "All have sinned " and need God's saving grace.

Sometimes it is not the world but it's the Christian disciple that opposes Christ. Remember Peter's response to Christ when Christ revealed that He would suffer and die at the hands of sinful men. Peter said, "Never, Lord. This shall never happen to you." And Christ responded, "Get Thee behind me, Satan," and explained to Peter that Peter did not have the "things of God in mind but the things of men." Have you ever been guilty of that? I have. Have you acted with your rational, humanistic thinking only later to comprehend that certain issue from God's perspective and realize the error of your ways? I have. What a difficult time for Christ! He knew He was to suffer a horrific death in but a few hours. In Gethsemane's garden Christ prayed to His Father with drops of bloody sweat on His brow. He agonized for deliverance from this horrible death. Peter's encouragement might have been a Satanic temptation. We always must understand that God's ways, God's thoughts, God's plans are not always the same as ours. We must not thwart or react against, but submit to, our Heavenly Father who is "for us."

Remember also another event. On the very night He was taken captive, at the Last supper, Peter rejected Christ's attempt to wash Peter's feet. But Christ's simple and firm reply was that unless Peter allowed Him to wash Peter's feet then, "you have no part with me." Peter's prompt response was then "wash my hands and my head as well." We must accept Christ's humble service to us. And once again His example has shown us how to live as servants to one another. His very life and salvation are acts of humble servitude. The Almighty Creator, the ever existent One, was marred by a vicious death. Unless we are willing to accept this service for us then we can have no part of Him or He of us.

We should not be surprised by opposition to Christianity and its followers. Peter reminds God's elect, "Dear friends do not be surprised at the painful trials you are suffering as though something strange were happening to you. But rejoice that you participate in the sufferings of Christ so that you may be overjoyed when His glory is revealed. If you are insulted because of the name of Christ you are blessed because the Spirit and the glory of God rest upon you." Then he further states that those who suffer according to God's will should commit themselves to their faithful Creator. (Note that the goal is the revelation of God's glory. There is no revelation of self. Note also that God is faithful. I Peter 4)

He tells us, "Therefore, since Christ suffered in His body, arm yourselves also with the same attitude." (Remember how He suffered unjustly physically and emotionally but was willing to suffer for good, the truth, and the Father's will?)

That mind of Christ was an attitude that obediently served at the will of the Father even sacrificially for others. (Phil 2:5) Christ gave Himself with joy because of the eternal relationship He had with the father. (Heb 12:2) Christ Himself said, "Blessed are you when people insult you, persecute you, and falsely say all kinds of evil against you because of me." (Matt 5:11) He also said, "Rejoice and be glad for great is your reward that is in Heaven." (Matt 5:12) He reminds his disciples in John 15:20 to remember the words he had spoken, "No servant is greater than the Master. If they persecuted me they will persecute you also."

Paul tells the Corinthians that the Apostles are truly suffering, "They have become the scum of the earth—the refuse of the world." But he also tells how they handled their suffering, "When we are persecuted we endure it, when we are slandered we answer kindly." (I Corinthians 4:12) Paul exhorts, "Bless those who persecute you, bless and do not curse." (Romans 12:14) He explains, "We rejoice in our sufferings because we know that suffering produces perseverance which produces character which produces hope." (Romans 5:3)

Clearly the suffering and persecution in question are not the result of personal acts of stupidity and misbehavior or are not because of our own personality disorders or agendas. It is the result of honoring God, of upholding His character and glory and of doing His will.

Opposition and suffering are part of Christendom's heritage. God's glory and Character are the focus of the attack by the "prince of the power" of the air. Christianity is in a sense a "counter culture."

Review the trials and fate of those listed in the honor roll of the victorious faithful found in Heb 11. Remember the testing of the Patriarchs, the Saints, the First century Christian. Why should it be any different for us? Read of the Apostle Paul and the major adversities in his life. Look at the Apostles' deaths!

We are warned that the Christian life is a battlefield. We are in a spiritual warfare that requires special armor and power to endure and progress. We are encouraged that even though this new life will be arduous, the power to run and finish this race is from a supernatural energy source.

We can expect the same treatment as our Christian Brothers and Sisters of History. Why? Because what is under attack is the Character and testimony of Christ. The end goal of the Christian life is to be conformed to the image of Christ. And that goal will be opposed for us personally as individual representatives of Christ as well as corporately as His earthly body, the Church. We deal with an ungodly system of thought and governance that does not understand or even consider the thoughts and rule of God. His life flows through us and his mind is to be in us. He was misunderstood. He clashed with the religious culture and politicians of his day. Why would it be different for us? We will not be attacked for doing good things. Society accepts and even encourages us to do neighborly and charitable endeavors. However, we all could name names of those maligned and politically opposed because of their moral stands. But compared to those under totalitarian/communistic rules we know nothing of opposition.

Once on a trip to Laos, our medical ream visited an ophthalmologist who was one of three in the country of Laos. He had spent time in prison and had been under house arrest for his Christian beliefs. We felt quite uncomfortable being there because he was obviously being observed by the authorities. We did not want to do or say anything that would further compromise his status. We should be grateful for our freedom to worship.

There are many personal stories of courage and victory. One Sunday morning while driving to the hospital to make medical rounds before Church, I listened to the radio and heard Ravi Zacharias tell the following story (as I remember it). He had been a chaplain in Vietnam during the war and had traveled that country extensively with a Vietnamese interpreter who was a Christian. After the Communist take over, Ravi lost contact with this fellow. A number of years later he received a phone call from California. It was this interpreter calling him. As they caught up with each others' news, the interpreter told Ravi what had happen to him after the North Vietnamese takeover. He had been imprisoned and treated poorly. One morning he reached the point where he felt he could no longer go on with God. God had not listened. It was too hard to continue a relationship. He decided that he would not continue to try, no longer would pray or mediate on God. The same morning he made this decision he was placed on latrine duty. While cleaning the bathroom toilets, he came across some toilet paper with writing on it. In order not to clog sewer systems, toilet tissue was placed in containers beside the toilet. The writing was a page from the New Testament. I don't recall what portion, but it was God's particular answer to this man's need at that time. He cried out to God in surprise and relief, "You couldn't even leave me alone for a day!" So this fellow requested to have latrine duty regularly after finding more of the New Testament the second day. Each day he received a new page of Scripture. After his release from prison, he learned that the Vietnamese soldier in charge had a new testament that he decided to use as toilet tissue. God provided this man's spiritual need in a most unique way. But the story did not end there. The interpreter and some friends planned a sea escape to Thailand. One night some Viet Cong came knocking at his door, barged in, pinned him to the wall, and demanded to know if he was planning to escape. He denied it. They left. He felt guilty about his lie. Severely oppressed by his lie, he told God if the Viet Cong returned he would tell them the truth. They came back and confronted him again. This time he told them he was planning an escape. And these Viet Cong responded, "We want to go with you." They were seamen and turned out to be the salvation of an eventual successful escape to Thailand.

But opposition is not just political ideological or physical. Our culture is filled with demands, images, words, and pressures that intimidate us, that make us question our faith, that distract us from eternal values that oppose or prevent a relationship with Jesus Christ, that muddy our thinking, and that diminish our ability to preserve our relationship to the Living Truth and to present Him in pure form to our own generation.

If we deny Creationism we deny the Creator.

If we deny absolute standards or values than we deny the very character of God and His work in us.

If we oppose the value of a life from its conception to its death than we become superior to the one who breathes life into us.

If we neglect family values and the family structure or if we accept cultural sexual mores and entangle our lives and finances in materialism then we effectively deny the Word of God and its power.

If we fail to fill our minds with only the things that are pure, lovely, virtuous and of good report then we are disobedient to God's plan for us.

And if we fail to stand strongly, if we fear, if we lack faith and disbelieve then we personally oppose His work in our lives.

Clearly there is a Christian strategy to opposition and suffering. That plan is based on our relationship to Christ. The trials of opposition are because of Him and for Him. He is not physically here, we are His stand-ins until He returns. We are to be His faithful servants because we love Him and because He is an integral part of our lives and character.

Christ, Himself, forewarned us to EXPECT opposition to evidences of a Christ-like character. When we endeavor to be salt and light in a world that desires darkness, decay, and an arrogant world system that does not wish Godly illumination and moral preservation, opposition will be a natural response to the Godly principles and the life of Christ who resides in the believer. Opposition will come when we take moral stands that are based on the moral law of God or on the teachings of the Word of God.

We are exhorted to ENDURE with patience and gentleness. GENTLENESS has been described as "strength under control." God is our strength and our confidence and therefore our CONTROL. Remember 1 Peter 4:17 exhorts us to commit ourselves to the faithful Creator who enables us to have the right responses.

Our attitude is to be JOYFUL, even in difficult circumstances, for the service of this wonderful King whom we love and about whom we testify.

Bashed and battered, oppressed and suffering The Church is negotiating its way through life's battles, but God declares us the Victors. We need His perspective. Christ has said that the Gates of Hell will not prevail against His Church. We are sometimes depressed and consumed by our failures. He envisions the Church as a conquering army. He knows the end result of this earthly travail: a redeemed, justified, glorified people—His perfect bride.

We understand ours is not a earthly **hope** but our **confidence** is in the Savior who prepares a place even now for those who have been victorious.

The Christian has died, has been buried and has risen again with Christ. He has died to self and as a result has found new life. The old Creation has passed away. The Tomb is empty. The new eternal Creation has risen within. Paul tells us in I Corinthians 15:54, "that the sting of death is sin and the power of sin is the law. But thanks be to God! He gives us the victory through Jesus Christ our Lord." Christ was victorious over sin, death and Satan, and His life flows within us. He gives us the power to live, to stand up and be strong in the face of adversity and opposition. He sees us as His children. He sees us as we will be someday, His righteous, holy and chosen people.

Controversy will swirl. We are to expect and to endure opposition with a gentle, joy-filled heart whose confidence is in the Lord of Hope, the object of our faith.

John tells us in 1 John 5:4, "Faith is the Victory that over comes the world." And then he says, "Who is it that overcomes the world? Only he who believes that Jesus is the Son of God."

The enemy of our souls continues to pick battles against Christ's ambassadors. The Captain of our faith has walked through the minefields of these skirmishes and is our ever present guide in life. The war is over! Victory was declared two thousand years ago in the life, death and resurrection of the Lord Jesus Christ. Our Hope is for that Glorious day when our redemption is complete and we stand perfected in His presence.

Little did His friends know the terrible drama of the next few days when they worshiped and honored Christ that night in Bethany two millenniums ago. A bright night fragrant with love would soon be marred by a dark denigration of God, who would in Holy anguish bear sin's painful burden for us. He knew His immediate future would be agonizing, physically, emotionally, and spiritually. Yet He did not complain.

What criticism, suffering, persecution or opposition will we cheerfully endure for Him? When the Christian faces opposition, his Hope is in the Lord. Listen to Him! He is ever present! He knows and understands! He is ever powerful! He has won the victory! Faith is the victory that overcomes the World!

Chapter 6
What Price Freedom?
Gal. 5:1
(Listen with a Free Heart)

Free at last,
Free at last,
Thank God Almighty,
Free at last.

The voice and image of the man that spoke those words will forever be etched in the memory of young Americans of the 60s. That decade began with optimism and a wonderful sense of idealism. Martin Luther King raised the national conscience of millions with his eloquent rhetoric. The morality of freedom became a lightening rod for debate and action. Our Nation had to face our ignorance, our complacency and prejudices that we had pretended to bury years before.

Our great country had been built on the belief of the equality of all men who deserved to have opportunities for fulfilling and decent lives within the boundaries of their intellect, their ambition and their abilities. People from around the globe have been welcomed and accepted into this nation where free thought and entrepreneurial ideas have brought many from despair to hope, from poverty to comparative riches, and from repression to freedom of movement, speech and religion and away from state control or tyranny.

The process of understanding the basis and morality of our freedom is ongoing. Not always understood and sometimes misinterpreted, freedom is based on moral law which is just as real as the natural laws that bind us. We are moral creatures as well as physical persons. We are created in the likeness of a moral being known as God.

He has directed us to the principles of life, or moral laws, which when pursued will bring us the happiness that we so much desire. But the boundaries of these principles have been continually blurred since we were placed in Paradise. Today the lines are not only blurring but are slowly being erased by such ideas as Political Correctness and the new "Civil Rights" as broadened and defined by the Civil Liberties Union and the Federal and State court systems that allow same sex marriages, pornography in the public libraries under the guise of freedom of speech, yet prohibit the display of moral principles in public places and in places of justice. They even make it illegal to talk about or teach about our Almighty Creator in public education. Without God the morality of freedom will be chewed and torn into bits of selfish license by groups interested only in their own agendas and not the moral good of society.

We began as a country of religious dissidents seeking religious freedoms. But even we, who sought relief from oppression, did not fully understand equality and the rights of other peoples and nations. Along with our successes came greed, corruption and abuse of power. We took advantage of others.

We wanted the great land that is now ours. But to gain it, we fought and shoved the Native American peoples to the West and eventually broke their spirit and relegated them to reservations. We entered into slave trade and abused African Americans for our commercial gain. Big companies have greedily mistreated their employees. Even after many years of these experiences we still have major problems with our biases, our prejudices and our concept of freedom.

Although we indeed are a melting pot of peoples, we have not fully accepted true equality of other fellow sojourners in a troubled land. This generation is much more accepting than even the generation of our parents when Jews had difficulty getting jobs and well qualified Asian Indians were given second rate jobs despite their obvious industriousness and intelligence. Yes, we are much more educated, and cosmopolitan, and tolerant than our Grandparents. In most ways that is good. But tolerance requires careful vigilance. One must strike a precautionary note. Freedom is precious and requires protection to survive. There must be protectors of the freedom. Sometimes the guardians of freedom are freedom's own worst enemy. Government is too big, too powerful, too intrusive, too cumbersome and expensive. It attempts to do more than it was intended to do. Courts are too liberal in their humanistic judicial minds. Schools are too emasculated to provide moral guidance. Parents are too busy, too in debt, too untrained and unmentored by the prior generation to know the boundaries of morality and civility. Unfortunately, we have become too politically and philosophically distracted to fulfill our obligations to freedom. We are losing it.

Our American history testifies to the fact that freedom comes at great price and sacrifice. Our wonderful Nation, with its cultural and social diversity, is great because of this freedom. After we began our country as a group of people seeking religious freedom, we struggled for relief from the tyranny of others and to become a sovereign nation of our own. The revolutionary war is filled with our national heroes. We have read of the hardships that our poor armies endured for the cause of freedom. We nearly wrenched ourselves apart during the convulsion of the Civil War. Eventually, freedom's cause liberated slaves and we began a long journey against prejudice and for racial equality. Our nation has championed and continues to champion freedom throughout the globe. We have experienced the repression of tyranny and know the preciousness and benefits of freedom and believe that all peoples should be free. The wisdom of our forefathers has kept us on track through an amazing Constitution, which is constantly being challenged and twisted by those who should guard it within the moral context in which it was framed. Politicians have lost focus. Their power is dependent upon blocks of people interested in their own agendas, whether it be pro-choice, homosexual rights, children's rights, religious rights, telemarketers' rights, or the rights of those felt discriminated against by age, race, sex, or lifestyle orientation.

Our freedoms and rights should be measured by the rights given us by God and the moral boundaries that He set. Love is the greatest ethic. Christ succinctly summed up this ethic, "Love God with all your strength and your neighbor as yourself." The Mosaic Law laid out specific guidelines which are principles of love, justice and righteousness. These principles have been under attack by subversive demands of individual groups who want license and affirmation to do their own thing without consideration to the whole of society. They twist and pull, fray and tear at the fabric of freedom.

Such issues as pro-choice, prayer in the schools, discriminatory claims due to age, race, sex, and lifestyle orientation need to be considered in the context of what is loving, just, and right. Freedom should not depend on the whimsy of conceited minds of judges who have political aspirations and know more than God.

For each of us freedom has its own personal set of names and faces and events that symbolize its meaning to us. The roll call of our heroes and freedom fighters would be too extensive to list. All subcultures of our American dream have their own heroes. There are so many that have exemplified the courage, resolve and faith on which this country was founded.

There were the Pilgrims and the early Indians who helped us survive our first year in the New Colony. Great Chieftains fought to preserve their nations. We proudly and gratefully remember great leaders, patriots, social architects, Presidents, spokesmen and military men and women. Thousands of heroes have died for freedom in the name of their country in known and unfamiliar places around this globe.

For some the word "freedom" brings back memories and smells of foreign places where wars were waged and liberating forces kept the peace. Those who did not go have read the accounts and seen the footage of land and air battles for Europe and Asia. We have seen the devastation. Some may have lived in terror under Hitler's Third Reich and barely survived the physical and mental devastation of POW or concentration camps. Some have walked angry roads and crossed Southern bridges in the 60s. Others may have traveled to or lived in communist countries and have seen or known first hand the lack of basic freedoms. There was no right to pursue happiness, free speech, and the freedom of religious worship.

We recall the battles of our more recent history: The Battle of the Bulge, the Beaches of Normandy, Hamburger Hill, Tet offensive of '68, the Gulf War, Baghdad. All these names resurrect sad and bitter memories. Yet as a country we stand tall among the nations. We have made many sacrifices in the name of freedom.

We all have visions of strange battle lines drawn by men and boys marching to the fife and drum. They stand facing their enemy countrymen, raise their muskets, fire point blank and reload for the next volley. Line after line topples in Gettysburg's beautiful fields where brother shed the blood of brother.

We feel the suspense as Paul Revere awaits the light in the North Church. That signal gives the message to the Massachusetts countryside of how the British will invade, "One if by land and two if by sea—"

We hold our breath as a drab, motley New England militia withstands the bright Red Coats. We envision again the rice paddies of Asia, the hot desserts of Iraq, Saudi Arabia and North Africa.

True freedom is gender and color blind. But it is painted Crimson Red with the brush of lives who have died for it. That is the price of freedom: sweat, sacrifice, and a flood of rich, American blood diluted with tears.

Some may put a face to freedom. There are faces of Generals such as Eisenhower, Patton, Washington or the visage of those who stood tall against wrong and for the right such as Abraham Lincoln. We picture our wise forefathers, Ben Franklin and Thomas Jefferson, or those who have fought ugly racial discrimination, Nelson Mandella, Martin Luther King. Winston Churchill faced the tyranny overtaking Europe. Perhaps the face of freedom is written on a local or national memorial. The Korean Memorial may cause you to whisper a name. A precious face may reflect from a V- shaped monument where the names of all the Vietnam war casualties reside. Maybe you remember that emotion filled image of brave men struggling to raise The Stars and Stripes on Iwo Jima.

Freedom is youthful, hope-filled faces bright with opportunities for those who wish to achieve, who eagerly exchange ideas and talents for advantages and success in areas of thought, in social good, in science, and in capitalistic ventures. It is the relaxed, happy countenance of those who do not know the fearful, controlling presence of a soldier on every street corner. It is the clear, unhesitant voice of dissent from those who do not fear tyrannical rule where one is watched and endangered for opposing the ruling power or receives retribution against their person or family for speaking freely. Freedom's face reflects from village church steeples that populate every New England town. It is seen in the proud, thoughtful look of the man and woman at the ballot box silently and powerfully speaking their voice. Perhaps freedom is best felt by swelling hearts and watery eyes as the "National Anthem" is sung and the flag proudly waves, cheered on by the unrestrained winds of our country. I, personally, will always remember boys becoming men too early, wearing combat fatigues, carrying weapons, and risking their lives in foreign jungles to keep free a people they did not know or understand.

Having grown up in Maine in the 1940s and early 50s, I first began to see freedom through the eyes of a small town American lad. For the first thirteen years of life I lived in a town with a population of three hundred and fifty souls. Half the town were relatives. It was a time of security, love, community awareness, and a sense of freedom. People helped others, there were community fund raisers, bean suppers, pies, town skits, Christmas plays, and town meetings that even as children we attended with our parents and learned about local government. There was a small church where my brother and I rang the bell every Sunday morning. So much of our early life revolved around that small church and the wonderful freedom of worship. Even in the public schools we sang patriotic songs, learned Bible verses and had weekly Bible flannel graph lessons. I remember the proud faces of town veterans poured into their old uniforms proudly marching in Memorial Day parades. A car marked with a gold star led the parades. My mother explained that family was being honored for having lost a son in the war. An old man, who was probably all of fifty and was actually my father's cousin's husband, proudly wore his WWI uniform with its wide brim scout-like hat. He was known as "Stub." Every Christmas his wife gave him a new saw. Before the new year was in, he had sawed off another finger. I remember being curious about him but feeling very proud of him.

My first real recollection of war was VJ day 1945. That day I heard shouting and bands playing and bells ringing. My father told me that we were celebrating the defeat of Japan. My dad worked at the Bath Iron Works in Bath, Maine. My uncle navigated bombers in Asia. My father-in-law to be became an ace pilot over the fields of France and Germany. As I grew older, I actually knew young men who fought and died in the Korean War and knew the sadness that freedom extracted from families and friends. In the 60s, my brothers joined the Navy. I lost friends my own age in the Vietnam conflict. In 1971 war became a reality in my own life as a Medical Officer on tour in Vietnam. I knew what it was like to be anxious and fearful of an unknown enemy. I saw faces seven and eight years younger than myself struggling with loss, fear, injuries, and burdened with guilt. Young, scarred, wounded, dying boys. The price of freedom raised some questions in my mind. The enemy, trained and indoctrinated by ideologies foreign to our thinking, were also young boys who had homes and families. They were fodder at the mercy of a government that wanted only to control them, use them, and did not care about them. I was saddened but not disheartened entirely because I could see that freedom was worth keeping. Now that I am a senior citizen, the face of freedom looks so very young. The names of the places are new, Afghanistan, Iraq and African countries. But the faces are the same—those of relatives, and friends' and neighbors' children. And the pain is as wrenching and awful. Encouragement and sometimes mourning are now the support I can give to these young, brave men and women who continue the fight for peace for others and freedom from terror for us. However they must be supported for keeping American free by standing up for what is right.

The other night I awoke with these words beating in my head, "Stand fast in the liberty wherein Christ hath made you free." (Galatians 5:1) This is the King James wording. The NIV states it a little differently, "It is for freedom that Christ set us free." I began to think about freedom and all its different facets. The context of this verse is that the Galatians had stopped resting in the grace of God. They were resorting back to a performance religion where works were important to their salvation. One of the key verses of Galatians is 4:8-9: "By grace are ye saved through faith...." Salvation is God's gift to us. Our works can not earn it. We are all on the same level ground with no cause for pride or self promotion. It is God's provision for us; we need only to accept it. Earning it is not an option.

Romans chapter six makes it very clear that the believer is not under the requirement of the law but is subject to a new law, the law of the Spirit. Furthermore, the believer's sinful nature has died with Christ and is now alive unto God. Self, sin, death, and the law no longer have condemning power over the lives of the Christian. This new life with the indwelling Christ gives us access to a relationship with the Father. We become his children and inherit eternal life (our hope).

However, there are boundaries to our newfound freedom. We have become slaves to righteousness. **Freedom has**

boundaries! Freedom implies that someone or something has had control. There is a desire for and a release from the control or boundaries imposed by that something or someone. It may be the tyranny of one's own government, or that of a foreign power, or of some vice or addiction, or some indebtedness, or some personal need or drive. It might even be a desire to be free from the boundaries set by God. In His wisdom and love He created us with a will and the ability to choose, to make decisions whether good or bad. He did not leave us without guidance. Sometimes we choose what we think is freedom but find it to be bondage. As we push and penetrate through our moral boundaries, natural self rises in power, arrogance, self-righteous rationalization, and self realization demanding that we do what **we** want. Self demands its right to be supreme and free from the influence of God, to step outside the boundaries of His benefits and blessing.

Whether we like it or not, we have boundaries. There are boundaries of time with its earthly beginning and end. Physical boundaries of space and places confine us. Unchangeable natural laws govern the way our universe operates. We are framed within boundaries of personality and capabilities. We have moral boundaries. Some may be set by societies. Ultimate boundaries are set by a just, loving and righteous God who understands what is best for His created creatures. He can not be anything but Himself. And we were created in His moral image. There are lines we should not cross. In Eden, Adam and Eve stepped beyond the line. We were free and did not know it or accept it. We chose to exercise our will. What we thought would be freedom became bondage.

We must acknowledge the source of our freedom as God. We are debtor to those who have directed us to an understanding of God and His love for us. Scripture is filled with examples of those who overstepped God's guiding boundaries. Adam and Eve were enticed beyond the boundaries, and we have never been able to return to the garden. Noah's generation drowned in their selfish, immoral freedom rather than live a harmonious life with God. The Israelites died in disgrace as nomads rather than eat the sweet fruits of obedience in a wonderful land prepared by God. *Jeremiah 43 tells of Israel's subsequent failures as they chose again to ignore God. He gave them their "freedom" and the consequences were prolonged sadness and exile.* David spiraled from one moral failure to another and reaped severe penalties for his sin of disobedience to God's moral laws. The young lawyer, who was a good moral person, went from Christ unsatisfied and unsaved because he lacked willingness to meet the standard of freedom. He chose wealth as his god. He put materialism above his relationship with God. The religious rulers who rejected the Lord Jesus Christ chose rules, regulations and legalism over the revelation of the Messiah. Their authority was threatened. They were blinded by selfish fear and did not see the lowly man of truth. They loved the perks of earthly prestige over the vast wealth of Heavenly glory. They were hypocrites described as white washed sepulchers. They deluded themselves into believing they knew God, but they sold His precious Son for thirty pieces of silver.

Yes, we can have our freedom from the blessing of God but discover ourselves in bondage—slavery to self, sin, the deceitfulness of the "things" of life and other satanic distractions. **We need to put our selves in the context of who we are. Read Isaiah 42.** God has rights to us. He is our Creator. All good and perfect things originate in Him. He has bought us from the slave market and given us freedom from that nature that counteracts His will. He has given us the great rights of harmony with Him and to be who we were meant to be. But there are many subversive counter-influences that tug at us, lure and persuade us, and dissuade us from our rights. Humanistic and vain philosophies masquerade as superior intelligence and argue:

- that we do not need God, if indeed there is a God at all,
- that God has no relevance in our education or our politics,
- that we need to give peace a chance (even though we do not know what love is), and
- that we can determine our own fate.

Although that thought has some truth to it, intelligence will not determines our fate. Our choices will. Temporal decisions are frequently based on impulse and emotion rather than on reason. History indicates that we have not improved our chances for a good conclusion to our existence as a world.

God, Himself has boundaries, not of time because He is infinite, not of power because He is the Almighty Omnipotent One, not of knowledge because He is omniscient. But as a moral being He is bound by morality, purity, holiness, love, justice and righteousness.

The hero of our freedom is the Lord Jesus Christ who won our freedom in the shame and seemingly defeat at the Old Rugged Cross. Yes, **Christ has made us free**. That freedom is from bondage of self, sin, death and the law. We are to stand in that liberty.

He came purposefully to restore us to the Father. Mysteriously announced by Heavenly hosts who declared great joy at His birth, the Prince of Heaven was born into the poorest of circumstances. Born in a stable, laid in a manger of hay, He grew up as a lowly carpenter's son. Destitute, he trod around the dusty land of Israel for three years with an unlikely band of followers who did not fully understand Him but professed confidence and belief in Him. Tragically, in His hour of greatest need for their friendship, they deserted Him. With our mind's eye we see a disgraced vagabond hanging crucified between two criminals on a hillside cross in a surreal scene darkened by the absence of the Heavenly Father who had once announced Him as the Savior of the world and declared approval of this Only Begotten Son. Seemingly a farce now, Christ was mocked and scorned by the religious leaders and soldiers and those viewing the death of our Savior. Certainly there was no Victory there. Yet if we peer deeper into this sad moment in time, **we detect the smoke of a raging battle.**

The Prince of Darkness, the prince of the power of the air, has unleashed his hellish demons. Prejudice, hate, pride, legalism, fear, selfishness and greed fly in the face of the lovely Prince of Peace.

The hordes of Hell rage against the restrained Heavenly Hosts.

The roaring lion who seeks to devour those who love the Lord has declared war against the Lion of Judah.

The false angel of light fights to extinguish the Light of the World.

Lucifer, the physically beautiful one, opposes the Lilly of the Valley whose visage is marred with painful suffering.

The fallen star screams his insults at the Bright and Morning Star.

The deceitful, slimy serpent crawls on its lowly belly and strikes venomously at the Almighty God who resides in the lofty heavens.

The cunning usurper riles against the Captain of our Faith.

The master masquerader performs his wicked work against the Master of the Universe.

Acrimonious taunts against Christ waft in the air of sulfurous brimstone and the death smell emanating from the Pit. The sickening smugness of the religious leaders is the face of pride that God abhors. The painful Crown of Thorns pierces not only the King of the Jews but the King of the Universe. Dirty spikes and spears of careless soldiers barbarously pierce the pure Lamb of God.

Beneath the black, wicked colors of this scene, lies even a deeper story of a life full of joy knowing that this day was the culmination of a great mission given by the Heavenly Father to His Son. A mission so important it had been decided upon before time started and could be accomplished only by Himself. He finished life full with the loving anticipation that He could return soon to His Father. It had been a Life of Love so deep we can not comprehend it, and a Perfect Life that became sin so that we might someday wear His pure robes of righteousness.

The scene is temporarily dark until lit up with radiant knowledge of Heavenly love that cannot be understood but will not let us go once it is received.

There is joy in heaven where one soul was added. The thief on the cross was promised Paradise that day because of his belief in the Lord. There was joy in Heaven because another soul entered the Kingdom of God. The Centurion recognized and acknowledged that Christ was indeed the Son of God. Do you suppose he was among the soldiers that had experienced God's overwhelming power and had been suddenly thrown to the ground the night before the Crucifixion when they marched against Christ in the Garden?

Our victory was won on the cross. The astounding proof of that triumph and the basis of our eternal Hope came three days later. At the empty Tomb the Angel announced, "He is not here.

He is risen." The "Victory over Death" bells have been ringing ever since.

How does one appropriate this freedom? By God's grace. It is a gift. But it must be chosen and be guarded, protected from the enemy that would rob it from us. That is where the "Stand Fast" in the liberty comes in. Be strong in the faith. To be strong we must equip ourselves for battle. Scripture and experience clearly reveal that we are in a spiritual warfare. God provides the necessary armor.

The helmet of Salvation protects the mind where the will operates. The mind is where belief becomes reality, and where faith sees and works itself out in practical ways.

The breastplate of righteousness covers the heart with the righteousness of Christ. Our righteous living flows from a heart in love with Christ, and God sees our inner life through the protective work of Christ.

The belt of truth girds us, holds us within the boundaries of God's Truth. It is the revealed Word of God. Christ and His character keep us contained in the image of Christ.

Our feet are fit with readiness to take the Gospel of peace. Blessed are the warriors for Christ who battle against the gospel of discontentment that separates us from God. Blessed are the soldiers who proclaim the gospel that gives mankind Peace with God.

The shield of faith protects us from flaming arrows that would ignite and turn our spiritual lives into smoke. The firm belief that God is real, vital, indwelling, loving, caring, trustworthy, eternal and wants us to be with Him protects us against the suffering, unanswered questions, pain and injustices we see and feel now.

The sword of the Spirit is the Word of God. It is quick and powerful and cuts to the core of issues of life, slices the vain delusions of self righteousness and lays open the very sores of personal moral failures and sins that ulcerate and infect our thoughts and weaken us. It allows the cleansing, healing work of the Spirit to effectively strengthen us.

Prayer is our communication with our concerned and ever available Commander who reveals His strategy for our lives. We can know and do His will.

Caleb, at eighty five years of age, was prepared to fight for the special portion of land God had given him years before. He trusted God for the future. If we know God, we not only believe in His promise of an eternal future with Him but will be willing to fight for, to appropriate, and to keep what God has given us. The Christian life is a battle, a race to the finish, and we need the strength of God to get through the battle to reach the finish line.

When I was a young boy, a visiting pastor told a story to our small Sunday school class about a little boy who was in a race and was getting very tired. He started to pray and was heard as he crossed the finish line, "You put them up, Lord, and I will put them down."

God has provided the equipment and the power. Our job is to wear the uniform and depend upon the person and power of Almighty God. This dependence and relationship was demonstrated vividly in the victorious life of Christ

who had authority over disease,
who claimed spiritual authority to forgive sins,
who calmed and healed the emotionally wounded, and
who spoke and nature responded.

He controlled all the realms of our human existence. In the parting moments before ascending into the heavens, He encouraged and energized His disciples with the revelation that all power and authority had been given unto Him.

The source of freedom is God Himself.
He loved us and created us by His choice.
To be free by the power of our choice.
He bought us back to be Free by His choice.
It is our choice to accept that Gift..
The boundaries of freedom are based on the morality of love and justice and righteousness.

The principles of freedom are based on God's moral laws for us.

The price of freedom was the crimson stained sacrifice of Christ as the only perfect fulfillment of the righteous requirements of the law. He demonstrated unconditional agape love, took our punishment, and paid the price of justice for our sins.

The face of freedom is not a visage that we know but is the character of Christ who is the truth of love, righteousness and justice. The truth shall make us free. Acceptance of Christ's work for us makes us free from self, sin, the law and death. We now see through a glass darkly, but we will see Him face to face when our personal battle is over.

The place of freedom is in repentance at the foot of the Old Rugged Cross.

The declaration of freedom is the gospel of Christ.

The battle for freedom is ongoing and requires aggressive protection with prescribed implements. If we do not protect our personal Faith carefully, we will be ineffectual warriors that limp wounded and traumatized across the battlefield of our spiritual lives.

God in His wisdom and love has made us free.

Stand fast in the liberty wherein Christ has made us free.
Freedom is His great work of grace.

Listen.
Hear it?
A song of the Redeemed.
Not even angels can sing it!

Free at last,

Free at last.

Thank God Almighty

Free at last.

Printed in the United States
23909LVS00001B/275